Of Humankindness:

Beyond the Field's Edge

Les Amis

Translated by S. Pluháček

Copyright © 2019 by Les Amis
All rights reserved
ISBN-13: 978-1082552403

Cover art "Blue Dandelion" by K.K. Pluhacek
Design by Carlye Elizabeth Thornton

CONTENTS

Of Humankindness   9

Hands   37

Philosophy: of agri-culture   47

The Wasteland Grows   71

Beyond the field's edge   105

Of Humankindness

I. Forever unsettled. And forever unsettling. The human condition. Solicited by a wonder more profound than any question. An insatiable hunger aroused. A desire without bounds awakened. Drawn toward a fathomless mystery. With one another. Sojourning along the way. Learning how to care, learning how to dwell.

Forever unsettled. And forever unsettling. This human condition. Of sharing. A sharing of nakedness, a sharing of fragility, a sharing of dependence. Not qualities or attributes of some subject or substance. Shared. And with this sharing set out along the way toward humankindness. A sharing that brings us forth in bringing us together. Thus not a sharing of our own doing, our own making. Not a sharing within our power. And yet a sharing in which we share.

An elemental sharing. A sharing of the elemental. Blood and breath. Warmth and nourishment. A sharing not reducible to the sharing of things. A sharing through which things emerge. A sharing through which there arises place and occasion for the appearing of all that is.

II. And yet somehow settled. At home. At home in the very unsettling—sharing—of existence. At home through caring. With these others. Here and now. Not here and now with these others. But with these others. And hence here and now. Not in a world (and) with these others. But with these others. And hence in a world. The *with* preceding the *in*. The *with* holding and holding together the *in*.

Nearer to one another than to any thing. Sharing with one another before and beyond being alongside any thing ready to hand. Sharing the warmth of a home between us. And in this way a world opens and unfolds.

Cradled by these hands. Suckled at this breast. Sharing the warmth of these hearts. Before even the stars and the seasons, we are roused and raised up by hearts and hands. We find our way by way of hearts and hands—a way of sharing and caring, and perhaps even a way of love. We belong to sharing and caring before and beyond any possibility of their belonging, like possessions, to us.

This primordial joining of hands and hearts, of flesh and spirit, a binding and bonding with one another. An originary belonging. A primordial ethos, a primordial art, a primordial religion. A faithfulness to the mystery that solicits us.

III. But recently—these past 12000 years—settled otherwise. Sedentary. Domesticated. Settled in advance. Residing in the house, alongside all it houses. The pressing throng of beings. The din of the world. The weight of the world. Absorbed by concern for the house and all it houses. Habituated to such concern. Accommodated to such concern.

Perhaps the settling of who we are and how we ought to live is as old as humankindness itself. But whether or not our settling is that old, the settling of who we are and how we ought to live took on new forms and intensified with our sedentary existence. First, our settling took the form of setting aside and settling alongside some more or less bounded portion of the earth. Our wandering, although it did not altogether cease, was greatly circumscribed, confined, even domesticated. We found ourselves walking along well-worn paths, paths laid out in advance of our sojourn, laid out between the here and there of our journey. And even before we found our footsteps to be drawing or following furrows in a field, a certain back and forth had settled over our existence. Second, our settling took the form of setting up and settling within houses. Our laboring, although it did not altogether cease, was put to work in the building and maintaining of more or less durable houses. And our attention was drawn—indeed, it was directed, even commanded—toward the house and all it housed. For the house and settling within the house allowed for a great proliferation of things. Our hands—and even our hearts—became preoccupied with the manufacture and use of things. Our relations to the earth, to one another, and even to ourselves became increasingly mediated—even *dominated*—by the house and all it housed. Third, our settling took the form of setting up and accommodating ourselves to the logics and economies of this sedentary existence. Our sharing, although it did not altogether cease, was increasingly covered over and hidden away (often behind walls and doors) or put in the service of taking, giving, and exchanging. We found ourselves trading with one another—something we had long done, but now at the expense of sharing (not only by taking and appropriating what had been shared so that it might now be traded; not only by substituting relations of gift and exchange where formerly sharing abided, but by diminishing the sway of sharing throughout our existence). A settling of accounts came to dominate our existence, a settling greatly aided by a keeping count in the form of writing. This settling of accounts was a fixing (in advance) of the stories of our lives—the imposition, the inscription of a durability there where stability formerly prevailed.

***

Our houses are monuments and tombs of forgetfulness. In them we forget our essential nature.

***

With our sedentary existence sojourning has become confused with coming round again like Odysseus to the old hearthside from which we set out. Half our journey becomes a retracing of our steps. Our spirit of adventure becomes domesticated. Sojourning and dwelling come to stand at a distance from one another. Whereas formerly we erred now here, now there, yet were always and everywhere at home in the world, our home now becomes fixed around the house.

***

With our sedentary existence *ethos* is confused with *oikos*. This is an *oikos* filled with *ousia*—*ousia* calling for *nomos*, for assignment, for distribution. In this way, the sharing of ethos is confused with eco-nomy—the distribution of *ousia* within the *oikos*. In this way, the sharing of ethos is made to accommodate itself to the mediation—the taking, giving, exchanging—of things, of beings, of *ousia*. In this way, the sharing of ethos—a sharing of hearts and hands, a sharing of the elemental, and, yes, perhaps even a sharing of words—is taken to be reducible to a peremptory directive and rules (*nomos*) that say (*logos*) how man ought to live in a fitting manner. Sharing in the labors of caring for nakedness, fragility, and dependence is reduced to a saying of rules that govern a well-ordered household.

***

Primordially, ethics does not ponder the abode of man. Rather, it shares in the opening and unfolding of a home between us. It shares in the labors of caring for this home. It does not stand at a distance, thinking. It joins with others in elaborating this home.

***

Of Humankindness

In coming to reside in the house and alongside all it houses, the world becomes replete with things: the beings that belong to us, our possessions, the beings over which we have disposal, those things constantly attainable and at hand in and around the house. Residing within the house—where our dwelling becomes habituated to remaining in a fixed location, our comings and goings localized around thresholds, hearths, altars—we are surrounded by things and our attention is more or less absorbed by a concern for things. In this world, things are taken as given. Things and a world filled with things appear as given—that is, as established, unavoidable, necessary. The human condition becomes characterized by working upon things—producing and sustaining things, ordering and distributing things—and by speaking about and acting with regard to things.

But before and beyond this sedentary existence, and its world replete with things, there opens and unfolds a world of sharing; a world of attentive eyes and attentive ears—eyes and ears not absorbed by a concern for things but instead attending to one another; a world of supportive and guiding hands—hands not grasping some stone, some tool but instead extending toward one another; a world of warm and caring hearts—hearts not hardened like clay and iron but instead opening tenderly toward one another. In this sharing—in this world of hearts and hands, of eyes and ears—there opens and unfolds place and occasion for things and a concern for things, but a place and occasion never replete with things and a concern for things. This sharing, this world does not await any thing, is not filled by any thing, is not exhausted by any thing.

Of Humankindness

***

Settled into the house and surrounded by all it houses, it is easy to become bewitched and bedazzled by beings and their being ready-to-hand and present-at-hand. It is easy to take our settled existence for existence as such. It is easy to take existence for a standing in the clearing afforded by the household. But our human sojourn long precedes and profoundly exceeds our sedentary existence. Our humankindness is not confined to or accomplished by standing in the clearing of being and beings. And even within our sedentary existence, even within the clearing of the household and its being(s), we draw near and share in a sharing that precedes and exceeds our sedentary existence.

***

Settled into the house and surrounded by all it houses, our existence is so dominated by beings that it can indeed be difficult to discern the being of these beings—taking being for nothing, taking being, and beings, for granted. And yet there sways, even more difficult to discern and to appreciate, the sharing in and through which being and beings emerge, show themselves, unfold.

***

We are not first and foremost in the world in the sense that we deal in a concernful and familiar way with entities encountered within-the-world. Before and beyond dealing with things within the world we share a world with one another, with hearts and hands joined—sharing a between, sharing an ethos, sharing a home, sharing in the care of one another. In the sharing of this *with* there lie farness and closeness. If any farness is made to vanish, this occurs within the sharing of a *with*. If our spatiality shows the characters of bringing close and distancing, these are not to be understood first and foremost in terms of things and our dealings with things but in our sharing with one another. Before the farness or remoteness of any thing is made to disappear, before any thing is brought close, we share in a between-one-another. In this sharing, in this between lie all closeness and remoteness, all bringing close, all holding at a distance. Before we discover the remoteness or closeness of any thing, we share in a joining of hearts and hands in which there is place and occasion not only for this or that thing but for a world between us. If we "have" an essential tendency toward closeness, this tendency arises in and as our sharing, caring, and dwelling with one another before and beyond all things. Our most essential tendency is *not* toward closeness with things but with one another.

***

Sharing a home *with others*—within which our being at home is at home—precedes all being at home *in something*. The familiarity of things presupposes and follows upon a familiarity shared with others. If to know—whether as *techne* or as *episteme*—is to be entirely at home in something, to understand and be expert in it, this knowing as being at home *in something* presupposes sharing a home *with others* through and within which something can come to appear and matter to one who would know.

This familiarity, this home, this ethos shared with others (before and beyond all appearing, all revealing, all unconcealing) is taken up and taken over and then covered over by the house and all it houses; covered over by the ways of being, including the knowing of *episteme* and *techne*, that reside within the house and the world founded upon it.

The house and all it houses comes to domesticate and dominate the sharing of the home. This domestication and domination take the form of *giving* and *receiving*, take the form of economy.

***

We are not (first) *thrown* into the world, *delivered over to it*. We come into the world by way of open hearts and open hands. We are held and cradled in their caring embrace. And in this way we come to share in an ethos, and a world, in which we matter, in which our existence is an issue for others. Our existence only comes to matter to us—and through this mattering the things of the world can come to matter to us—through our sharing in an ethos, a world in which we matter to others.

***

It is only with sedentary existence that man clings always and only to beings. And it is only within this domestication that man thinks from beings back to beings with a glance in passing toward being. It is only within a settled, sedentary existence that the being of beings becomes an overriding concern. Before and beyond this settled existence it is not beings—the substance of our household—that lie closest. It is not beings to which man always and only clings. Rather, we cling to the breast and to the hand of others. And we bathe in the elemental. No doubt we also cling to "things" (not *ousia*, not beings, but what then?) before and beyond our settled, sedentary existence. But we do not cling *always and only* to beings. Deeper than beings and that clearing of being in which they appear lies an elemental sharing, a sharing of the elemental through which an ethos opens and unfolds, a world worlds. This is not an ethos or world filled with beings and lit up by the light of being(s). This ethos overflows with an abundance and warmth born of sharing. An elemental abundance.

***

The elemental is no thing.

***

Before and beyond the house, a house replete with things, there opens and unfolds a home shared between us; a home not gathered—neither first and foremost nor necessarily—by way of things; a home not filled with things, a home not dependent upon things, a home not exhausted by things. Before and beyond the house, there opens and unfolds between us a sharing of the elemental. Our home abides in this sharing.

***

Our labor primordially lies in sharing and is directed toward the elemental. Working and effecting may lie in being and be directed toward beings. But such working and effecting is grounded in labor and in sharing the elemental.

***

The drawing near and gathering of the home differs from the drawing near and gathering of the house. There stands a substantial difference between the one and the other. This is the substantial (*ousia*) difference of the *oikos*. The substantial difference of the *oikos* obstructs the sharing of the home.

In our sedentary existence, we draw and are drawn near, we gather and are gathered in particular ways—which is to say that the drawing near and gathering in and around the house are not universal. Nor are they essential to humankindness. The drawing near and the gathering in and around the house are dominated by things. They take place around things and by way of things. And even if before and beyond our coming to reside in a house we now and then gather around things, our drawing near and gathering are not *dominated* by things.

***

Foremost among the things by which drawing near and gathering are dominated are the walls, the threshold, the door of the house. Despite their unobtrusiveness, these mechanisms organize our drawing near and gathering in and around the house. And despite their lowly state, standing upon foundations that lie beneath our feet, they are transcendent with respect to what and who is gathered by way of them.

***

The house is a script that precedes and founds those other civilizational scripts through which our drawing near and gathering are organized, framed (as *oikos*). The organization of life by scripts and frames—the subsistence conferred upon organization by scripts and frames—is an articulation of the substance, the *ousia* of the house. The frame of the house—its foundation, its walls, its roof; its laying out and arranging of space, of time, of action—frames the more specific scripts through which our drawing near and gathering are delimited, bound, defined. Before and beyond our sedentary existence, there is neither script nor frame to organize our drawing near and gathering. This is not to say that there is no hand guiding our sharing with one another. But this hand holds no pen nor is it preoccupied with a hammer. It is a hand that holds, cradles, caresses. It is an open hand that shares and extends. Again and again for the first time.

***

With the advent of our sedentary existence—and the domination of existence by things, foremost among them the house and all it houses—the sharing in and through which things arise, emerge, and find place and occasion recedes, is covered over, becomes impoverished. Sharing is hidden, concealed in its articulation in and as things. Sharing is concealed behind the walls of the house. Within the economy of these walls, sharing is impoverished. Things come to stand in the place (and occasion) of sharing. A space and time of taking, giving, and exchanging things comes to dis-place the place and occasion of sharing, the sharing of place and occasion. This is not a sharing of things, a distributive sharing, but rather that sharing in and through which things might pass from one to another. This is a sharing of breath and blood, of hands and hearts; a sharing of nakedness, of fragility, of dependence; a sharing between, a sharing of the between one and another; a sharing not brought forth or articulated by one and another, but rather a sharing that brings forth one and another; a sharing in which we share and in sharing are brought forth.

This concealing and impoverishment is repeated and reinforced again and again with each attempt to confine and restrict the sharing of a home within the economy of a house. This means that the opportunity to thwart this reduction, this concealing, this impoverishment arises again and again. Enormous effort—drawn ultimately from sharing—must be expended to maintain the domination of existence by things, by beings and being, by taking, giving, receiving, exchanging. But even the most secure house, the most secure economy is riven with cracks, fissures, leaks. Its foundations and walls must be shored up and repaired again and again. And yet all these efforts are ultimately bound to fail.

***

The *ethos* of the home precedes the *ousia* of the house.

Of Humankindness

***

With sharing lies the very worlding of the world. [A sharing not reducible to nor equivalent to the worlding of the world. A sharing broader and deeper than this.] This sharing does not simply occur in the world; is not simply a component, an aspect, a dimension of being-in-the-world. But when things come to dominate our existence—and the world comes to take on the durability and independence of things—the worlding of the world through and with our sharing is covered over.

***

With the advent of our sedentary existence the home comes to be confused with the house. The home is set within the house, centered around the house, subjected to the logics and economies of the house. This is another way of saying that sharing comes to be confused with taking, giving, and exchanging; that sharing is set within the logics and economies of the house, centered around its logics and economies. Sharing is put to work in the service of setting aside and setting upon; in the service of extracting, storing up, trading back and forth—often with an eye toward profitmaking at the expense of another. There is a subtle, largely hidden displacement of sharing by beings and being; a subtle, largely hidden displacement of sharing in the elemental by the taking and giving, the taking as given of beings and being.

The confusion of the home with the house is not simply a confusion with the house as shelter. It is also a confusion with all that the house shelters—all the household goods lying ready to hand for the work of and around the house. The proliferation of things kept ready to hand within the household introduces a durability into the lives of those who dwell within the house. Household goods come to mediate the togetherness, the sharing of those whose existence is preoccupied with them. The *durability* of these things comes to displace the *stability* of that sharing through which the home was brought forth again and again for the first time. The founding of the house covers over and impoverishes the sharing that must be renewed again and again. Sharing in the elemental fades into the background. The sharing of an ethos is covered over by the give and take of the house and all it houses. Still a sharing in the elemental abides—between birth and death; in health and in sickness; in friendship and in love.

***

With our settling within the house and its economy, sharing, as the element of caring, is increasingly abandoned in favor of taking and giving things. The taking and giving of things comes to dominate our care. This domination takes place around the house and all it houses. The world comes to be taken as one great storehouse, holding resources to be extracted, mined, worked upon. Care does not end when it "slips out" of its element, but it does become impoverished. Care becomes less than it might be in its becoming preoccupied with the taking and giving of things; in its becoming preoccupied with being and beings.

Still, even a care that safeguards our nakedness, fragility, and dependence through the making and use of artifacts intended to cover our nakedness or to armor our fragility remains a human care. But insofar as it fails to care for this nakedness as nakedness, to care for this fragility as fragility, this care fails to lead us toward the accomplishment of humankindness. It fails to lead us toward unfolding more fully our nakedness, fragility, and dependence. It may make of us a Titanic force capable of remaking the earth and engineering life, but it fails to lead us toward the flourishing of the most primordial dimensions of humankindness.

***

Sharing, as the milieu of caring, is impoverished by the economic articulations of caring. Sharing does not come to an end with such articulations, but it does become impoverished. We dwell, unavoidably, in sharing. But this does not mean that we dwell fully in sharing or that our dwelling accomplishes sharing.

***

Sharing shares forth humankindness. And humankindness, in turn, shares in myriad ways with this primordial sharing. Sharing is thus not the product of humankindness. There can be no appropriating or taking over of this sharing, our home, in and through which we primordially dwell. We can "only" share (however poorly) in this sharing.

***

Of Humankindness

The domestication of sharing resides in the domestication of the there, of being the there. The enduring presence of the house and all it holds (*ousia*) appears to hold open and maintain the there without us. The world, rather than opening and unfolding through the sharing of an ethos, stands there completed and ready to be inhabited. We find ourselves thrown into a world rather than coming to share the worlding of the world.

***

As a result of the confusion of home and house within our sedentary existence, homelessness comes to be experienced and understood in terms of the house and all it houses. Homelessness as a wandering away from (or a covering over or neglect of) that sharing through which the home abides—a sharing before and beyond the sharing of household goods—is forgotten in favor of a homelessness from being and beings. If, with our sedentary existence and its logics and economies of taking, giving, and exchanging, we have covered over or wandered away from our primordial home, our primordial sharing, our homecoming will not be accomplished by standing in the clearing of being and attending (by thinking and saying) to this clearing. The house of being is not the dwelling from which we have wandered away. A home of sharing awaits us beyond the clearing or horizon of being.

***

Of Humankindness

The failure of traditional humanisms to realize the proper dignity of man is not due to their reliance upon a metaphysics that thinks beings—including human beings—back to beings with a glance in passing toward being; a metaphysics that thinks the humanity of man with regard to an already established interpretation of nature, history, world, and the ground of the world. Nor does their failure rest in failing to ask about the truth of being. And thus the failures of traditional humanisms will not be overcome by climbing back down into the nearness of being; nor by determining the essence of man to lie in any ecstatic inherence in the truth of being. It is not by standing out in the openness of being that man is man. And it is not as the shepherd of being that man accomplishes the essence of his humanity. Humankindness is not realized through a rigor of meditation, a carefulness of saying, a frugality with words. Rather, humankindness flowers and bears fruit through sharing in the labors of caring for nakedness, fragility, and dependence. Through such sharing the world worlds. Through such sharing we care for the earth and for one another. And through such sharing we accomplish our humankindness. The failure of traditional humanisms has been due to their neglect of the primordial breadth and depth of humankindness.

IV. Toward a humankindness beyond the field's edge.

Humankindness shares in a nakedness, a fragility, a dependence that cannot be covered over, armored, or dispelled by any technical artifice or prosthetic device—although such machinations can impoverish our humankindness. Sharing—

sharing a there—precedes and exceeds the intervention of any technical artefact or setup. The there of an ethos shared between us; shared in the labor of caring with and for one another, a care that does not await and is not reducible to technical intervention. The technical takes place through and within the between of this sharing. It does not open and clear this between. It presupposes it. And although it may profoundly transform this between, it does so upon a ground that precedes and exceeds it.

Sharing abides. And yet its abiding is taken for granted. Its abiding is assumed (not as such, not resolutely) and put to work as gift, as exchange, as being. Sharing persists as being—as property, as household, as clearing and opening (of an expanse within the forest), as constant presence, as availability, as disposability.... To persist as being is not to flourish—nor is such persistence fulfillment or accomplishment.

Still, even in its being diminished and impoverished—as being, as gift, as exchange—sharing abides. That is to say, sharing is not exhausted in its being taken for granted. Every taking for granted, all granting, receiving, exchanging presuppose sharing.

***

Humankindness: naked, fragile, and dependent—and sharing in the labors of caring for this nakedness, fragility, and dependence. This nakedness, fragility, and dependence are our Epimethean inheritance. And such care is our primordial Promethean inheritance. These Promethean labors—and the sharing and caring through and as which they are elaborated—are not first and foremost, nor are they reducible to, the manufacture and manipulation of tools or things.

The dominant ways in which we have cared for our nakedness, fragility, and dependence these past 12000 years have been short on sharing and labor and long on exchange and work. As a result of this, our understanding of our Promethean inheritance has been rather narrow. It has been dominated by calculation and planning. It has privileged the durability of works over the stability of labors. It has become strongly associated with the cleverness of ruse and machination. It has come to be understood as a largely male and masculine enterprise. We have neglected and forgotten that more primordial Prometheus who was our mother, our provider(s) of care. The one whose hands held and cradled us, caressed and cleaned us, fed and nurtured us—before and beyond the throwing of stones, the manufacture and use of equipment, the articulation of any logos. The one whose heart safeguarded and warmed us before and beyond any shelter (made of stone or wood) and before and beyond any fire.

It is true that we are the offspring and the inheritors of that Prometheus known as a clever Titan. But our descent from this Prometheus is much more recent, far less primordial and profound than our descent from a Prometheus who was (and is) our mother.

**

We are, and have undoubtedly long been, cyborgs. Our existence has been wedded to technical artefacts for the past 3+ million years. And since the advent of agriculture—

and even more so with industrialization and digitalization—we have become increasingly dependent on these artefacts. Our entire "civilizational" apparatus has been founded and "raised up" upon this dependence. But our dependence upon technical artefacts is more profound than the conferring or securing of such benefits. These "artefacts" have become as much the maker of humans as humans can be said to be the makers of these artefacts. The there of our being-there is not simply a clearing in which technical objects might appear (and be used) as ready-to-hand or present-at-hand. The there has become as much an "effect" of technical objects as it is the clearing in and through which technical objects appear and function.

The question, however, is not whether we are (natural born) cyborgs. It is the extent to which we can be defined by and reduced to the cyborg nature of our being. The question is whether our humankindness exceeds (and perhaps in some sense precedes) our being cyborgs.

***

One of the greatest dangers facing us today (a danger we still do not face) is that our technical interventions become not merely the only way of caring but that they cover over or do away with the very nakedness, fragility, and dependence for which they are attempts to care.

***

To care for nakedness, fragility, and dependence is *not* to do away with them. Rather, it is to safeguard, nurture, and perhaps even cultivate them. We accomplish our humankindness through caring for our nakedness, fragility, and dependence. Such care is not merely some action that causes an effect. But nor is it merely a letting-be.

***

It may appear as if it has been decided once and for all in what our humankindness consists. These past 12000 years we seem to have decided, albeit not in a deliberate and thoughtful manner, that our humankindness is essentially Promethean. And not just essentially Promethean but completely Promethean. As if our destiny resided in the bestowal (upon ourselves) of techne and fire. Still, our Promethean inheritance and its possibilities tell us only part of our story. We tend to forget that the Promethean bestowal is directed toward an Epimethean mystery who stands there (and is not this standing already quite an accomplishment? must not its story also be told?) naked, unshod, unbedded, and unarmed. It is this mystery who is in a position (which is not simply nor first and foremost one of need, of indigence, of lack) to receive what Prometheus bestows. And this position is not simply one of reception—as if we were formless clay waiting to be shaped or empty vessels waiting to be filled. For this position is a consequence of our nakedness, fragility, and dependence. We do not receive these essential attributes in the same way we receive the (stolen) gifts of Prometheus. *We* do not receive them at all. They are far more primordially constitutive of who we are. We are who we are through sharing (in) nakedness, fragility, and dependence. These are not gifts bestowed upon us. They are not gifts that can be taken away from us. We share in them before and beyond any giving or taking—and it is this sharing that makes the giving and taking of any gifts possible.

***

We are the offspring of both Epimetheus and Prometheus: we are naked, fragile, and dependent (naked, unshod, unbedded, unarmed) and we share in the labors of caring for this nakedness, fragility, and dependence. These labors—and the sharing and caring through and as which they are elaborated—are not first and foremost (nor are they reducible to) the manufacture and use (manipulation) of tools or things. They are more primordial than that. We have not yet fathomed the depths of our humankindness. And thus we do not know who we might yet become. We do not know what we are capable of as naked, fragile, and dependent. And we do not know what we are capable of as clever and resourceful tool-using animals. Nor do we know in what ways our Epimethean and Promethean tendencies might be joined, wedded, woven together. One thing we can be sure of, however, is that these past 12000 years of sedentary existence in no way exhaust (or accomplish) our humankindness.

***

It is curious that philosophers, whose hands hold little more than a glass of wine, a cup of coffee, and occasionally a pen, envision the hand as holding tools for throwing, striking, and cutting. The hand that shelters and supports; the hand that holds and caresses; the hand that nourishes and nurtures; the hand that grooms and guides; the hand that points and shows; the hand that greets and bids farewell. Such hands, holding no tool, are forgotten by the philosopher—who has undoubtedly benefited greatly from these hands.

***

Human dignity consists in caring for that nakedness, fragility, and dependence through which we share in a world and in the worlding of this world.

***

Our task today is to free our care from a preoccupation with things into a more primordial safeguarding, preserving, and nurturing of our nakedness, fragility, and dependence. This is not simply a mundane, intra-worldly care—a care for humans distinct from other forms of care, such as a care for nature or a care for art. Rather, in this care the world worlds. The world opens and unfolds, sharing out place and occasion for all that is.

***

We are still far from accomplishing humankindness. We attend to our humanity in a largely one-sided manner, unfolding certain Promethean qualities while neglecting or shunning our nakedness, our fragility, our dependence. Not only do we fail to devote ourselves to unfolding more fully these

Epimethean qualities, but our care for our Promethean ones is narrow and superficial. The Prometheus with whom we are familiar is a consequence of our having neglected and forgotten our Epimethean possibilities. These Epimethean possibilities are not faults or lacks in need of Promethean supplementation. Such possibilities are not accomplished through a technical intervention that would cover them over or armor them with a prosthetic device. Our humankindness opens and unfolds through the sharing of them and we cannot flourish by neglecting, denying, or hiding (from) them.

We are so bewitched and bedazzled by certain Promethean possibilities, so blinded by the light of the fire we have "acquired," that we have become insensitive to and ignorant of our Epimethean possibilities—those embers of warmth from which a fire is lit. Who today even recalls these Epimethean possibilities? And along with them very different Promethean possibilities? Promethean possibilities not narrowly preoccupied with covering over and concealing (or distancing us from) our Epimethean possibilities, but with unfolding more fully these very possibilities?

***

Born into kindness. Not into a cold and alien world, but into the warmth of *these* hearts, the steadiness of *these* hands. Yes, born into humankindness. Born into a sharing in which we share. A sharing not given in advance. A sharing not of our own making. A sharing that opens and unfolds through our sharing.

Of Humankindness

Born into humankindness. And hence not thrown into the world. Cradled in *these* hands, suckled at *this* breast. Born into sharing. And hence not abandoned to the tyranny of what is already there. A mystery born into a mystery. There to unsettle what had appeared settled. And to settle anew alongside others into an ethos, a world.

Born into humankindness. And hence not simply into a world, but into the very worlding of the world. Into the sharing and caring through which a world is elaborated. [To elaborate a world is not to create—and certainly not to create out of nothing. But any question of (prior) creation only arises within a world elaborated. The givenness of a created world oddly presupposes sharing in the elaboration of a world.]

Born into nakedness, fragility, and dependence. And raised up with our nakedness, fragility, and dependence into humankindness. Not raised up so as to leave these behind, covering them over or armoring them, but to unfold them more fully into flourishing and accomplishment.

Born into kindness. Raised up into kindness—a kindness no matter how diminished, how impoverished. Our humanity abides in kindness. Our humanity unfolds most fully in kindness. The kindness of sharing, of caring, of loving. This is a kindness not merely *in* the world, not merely *of* the world. Not merely a kindness concerned with the things of the world. Rather, a kindness through which the world opens, unfolds, abides.

Of Humankindness

Raised up into humankindness. Coming to share in the opening and unfolding of a home, of a world. Raised up not simply into the ways of the world, but into the very opening and unfolding of a world. Raised up into sharing more fully with others the joys and sorrows of life. Raised up into a tenderheartedness, faithful to the tender heart with which each one of us was born.

Hands

Hands: opening and extending a world—before and beyond the back and forth of any thing; sharing the elemental—before and beyond the giving or receiving of any gifts; laboring to care for our nakedness, our fragility, our dependence—before and beyond any works.

***

     Hands not dependent upon the light (of being) to sense, to learn, to instruct.

     Hands sinking into earth and world before and beyond any concernful absorption with things ready to hand or present at hand.

***

Of Humankindness

Hands holding the elemental. Hands sharing the elemental. Hands conveying sustenance to the mouth of another. Hands joined with (and joining) hearts—an originary art, an originary ethics, an originary religion—before being yoked to the intellect.

***

The labors of these hands wordlessly elaborating primordial prayers. Such labors—even in spanning a distance between here and there, between one and another—deepen the fecund mystery of the human sojourn, of world, of divinity....

***

Hands: laboring before and beyond all works. The elemental all around and shared between. No equipment to be put to work. No thing ready to hand. No thing present at hand.

The labor of hands. A labor curiously hidden, neglected, forgotten in the background of our concerns and our dealings with things. Yet without this labor—that is, without sharing and caring—there would be no world in which our hands might concernfully set about any work.

The arc of a thrown projectile, the flash of a hammer striking its target, the opening and unfolding of the knife's cut: all such actions presuppose an ethos and a world opened through the primordial labor of hands—both our own hands and, even more so, those of others.

Our works have failed to reveal, to illuminate, to lay out the labors on which they rest and upon which they are raised up. Indeed, our works have served to cover over and conceal such labors—even when these labors occur in plain sight. The works of our hands—in lighting up what shows itself in the opening expanse of their movements, in drawing the attention of our eyes—blind us to the labors from which they draw their inspiration and their sustenance.

***

Before our hands throw or strike or cut, they pick and scratch and rub. They caress and comfort. They groom and guide. They hold and carry. They nurse and nourish. They support and soothe. They bind and join. They beckon and welcome. And it is by way of such care that our hands might later come to seize some stick or grasp some stone and make a tool out of it, using it to throw, to strike, to cut.

Our hands begin their labors of humankindness long before becoming involved in the work of any tool. These are the labors of sharing and caring. And as a result of these labors, we become *who* we are and not simply *what* we are.

***

Of Humankindness

Despite the rather recent identification of man as a maker and user of tools—and the more narrow association of tools with weapons for throwing, for smashing, and for cutting—the humanity of humankind precedes and exceeds the manufacture and use of tools and lies deeper than the deploying of tools as weapons. The humanity of humankind lies much closer to the earth and to that sharing and caring through which a world primordially comes forth.

The hands that are capable of manufacturing and using tools are not simply given. Such hands have been raised up and made capable through the power and discipline of sharing. Such hands have shared in the sharing of the elemental—an elemental that is gathered and collected. That is, an elemental that is shared. For gathering and collecting are not first and foremost a taking, an acquiring and appropriating of some thing(s) that can then be given, distributed, exchanged. Gathering and collecting are ways of sharing in the elemental abundance of the earth. And they are ways of sharing forth this elemental abundance. They share in sharing.

The hands that are capable of manufacturing and using a tool have been cared for (cradled, caressed, comforted) and provided for (nursed, nourished, nurtured) long before such manufacture and use. Whatever capability these hands may have is grounded in this care and provision. It is such care and provision that are primordially Promethean. They open and clear a future within which there is place and occasion for the arc of a throw to disclose the possibilities of a world. They open and clear an ethos within which there might be elaboration and explication.

***

Why privilege the image of a hand throwing a rock or a spear—a projectile whose arc would supposedly open the space and time for a world? A world precedes any hand taking hold of some rock or some stick and thereby making a tool of it. Do not the caring hands that reach out to share the elemental with another open and span a distance, a between without the need of a tool or a weapon? Do not the hands extending between mother and child, hands extending across generations, open place and occasion for the stability (which is not equivalent to the durability) of a world? Do not the hands exploring and caressing the bodies of those who will be friends and lovers open place and occasion for a dialogue (often not in need of words, often beyond words) between worlds?

How much of our world—even our technologically saturated world today—remains beyond the reach of any tool? How much of our humanity precedes and exceeds the use of any tool? How much of our sharing in the opening and unfolding of place and occasion for the appearing of all that is precedes and exceeds the handling of any tool or equipment?

***

Neither humanity nor the world is born(e) or brought forth by hands that would forge a strange and estranging kinship with and between things. Not only are such hands insufficient to bring forth humanity, they are not simply nor are they straightforwardly necessary for the humanization of humanity. Although it may be true that such hands were necessary to bring forth humankind such as it is, it is not necessary that humankind be such as it is for it to be human.

***

Our sojourn thus far in no way exhausts the possibilities of humankind(ness).

***

Our hands accomplish much more than the manipulation of things. And it may even be that the manipulation of things limits or stunts other, more accomplished possibilities of our hands—not to mention the limitation, the stunting, the hardening of hearts that can result from a preoccupation with the manipulation of things.

***

Any connection *to* things presupposes the *with* of a sharing and caring before and beyond the reach of things.

***

It may be true that the transformation of what is standing and lying around into usable equipment can only begin when a hand reaches for things and finds them ready to hand, or makes them ready to hand. But it is not the case that such a transformation is the first act of world-production.

A world opens, pulsates, and unfolds before any hand handles any thing—and certainly before some thing is transformed into usable equipment by the work of some hand. And a world is sustained before and beyond the introduction of some (durable) thing. In the caring hands extended between one and another, a world worlds. Such hands need not hold any thing. And thus we must think the world and the worldhood of the world without any thing—and certainly without any equipment—ready to hand.

***

Perhaps even readiness-to-hand and equipment have nothing to contribute as ontological clues in Interpreting the primitive world; and certainly the ontology of Thinghood does even less (*Being and Time*, 113).

***

Hands: searching, gathering, and collecting before and beyond the logics and economies of agri-culture.

The association of gathering and collecting with the taking and appropriating of what has supposedly been given—as well as with any subsequent distributing, giving, or exchanging of what has been taken or appropriated—is a consequence of the privileging of tool use (of work and works) as the defining characteristic of human being. And this privileging goes hand in hand with an agri-cultural self-understanding of human being.

The logics and economies of agri-culture—which are rooted in the soil of agri-cultural existence—are logics and economies of taking as given, of giving as present. Such logics and economies grow out of the practices and habits of extracting, isolating, dividing, storing up, distributing, domesticating.... Though these logics and economies, as well as the practices and habits from which they grow, are grounded in a sharing of elemental abundance, they articulate this sharing in terms of taking, giving, and exchanging. Hence, the sharing of searching, gathering, and collecting are understood in terms of taking, giving, and exchanging.

***

These past 12000 years our hands have been so filled and preoccupied with the making and use of things that today we can scarcely imagine our hands and their handiness before or beyond such making and use. Nevertheless, our hands can accomplish our humanity without taking hold of any thing.

These past 12000 years our lives and our world have become so filled, so saturated, so dominated by things—things understood in terms of tools, equipment—that we cannot imagine a world beyond these things. And yet a world of humankindness precedes and exceeds these things.

***

Hands

Hands holding hands. Hands holding (on to) one another before holding any thing.

***

Humankindness shares in nakedness, fragility, and dependence. And humankindness cares for this nakedness, fragility, and dependence with the labor of hands and hearts—that is, through sharing the labor of caring for our nakedness, our fragility, our dependence. The use and manufacture of tools have long been part of such care and concern, but this concern is not reducible to tool use (our hands are handy for much more than grasping or throwing some stone, some thing) nor can this use be understood outside the context of its being coupled to our nakedness, fragility, and dependence. Our humanity begins to arise and abide before and beyond the use or manufacture of tools. And our humanity is not accomplished by the use or manufacture of tools.

***

Yes, our hands can do more than throw a stone or guide a plough—and much, much more than press a button or manipulate a device. The labors of our hands share in opening an ethos, a world before and beyond the arc of any projectile or the bounding of any field. In the open hands extended between one and another—a one and an other brought forth through the opening and openness of hands—the world first worlds. It worlds as ethos, as hearth, as place and occasion for sharing the warmth of hearts, the joining of destinies (a joining not bringing together two or more who previously stood apart, but rather bringing forth through and within a bringing together). In the tender caress, in the sharing of the elemental, a world—an ethos—opens and unfolds. It is through and within this opening and unfolding that a hand can grasp and throw a stone or hold and guide a plough. It is through and within this opening and unfolding that we can set about our labor and our work—a labor and work that do not await the seizing of a stone or the handling of a tool in order to share in the opening and unfolding of a world.

***

Hands: opening and extending a world—before and beyond the back and forth of any thing; sharing the elemental—before and beyond the giving or receiving of any gifts; laboring to care for our nakedness, our fragility, our dependence—before and beyond any works.

Philosophy: of agri-culture

Socrates: Let us imagine a city from the beginning. A city comes to exist because none of us is self-sufficient. We each have many needs we cannot satisfy. And such needs are the real creator of our city. The first and greatest of these needs is to provide food in order to sustain life. The second is for shelter, and the third is for clothes and things of that sort. All of these necessities will be provided best if each person contributes to the commonweal that work for which they are most well-suited and is freed from the other kinds of work for which they are less well-suited. Of course, this will mean that the farmers who produce our food will need metalworkers to produce hoes and ploughs and other agricultural implements. And the builders of houses will likewise need tools produced by others who are best suited for such work. So our city will have a sufficient number of citizens to provide for its needs.

    If we look at what sort of life people will lead who have been provided for in this way, we will see that they make food, wine, clothes, and shoes—as well as all the equipment necessary to provide themselves with these things. They will build houses and wear simple clothes. They will live unpretentious, honest, and reserved lives, producing no more children than their resources allow. They will live in peace and good health, passing on similar lives to their children and their children's children.

But if for some strange reason people are not satisfied with such a life and instead desire more than what this life provides, let us imagine the origins of a luxurious city too. And that may not be a bad idea, for in this way we might see how justice and injustice grow up in cities. Yet the true city, in my view, is the one we have just described, the healthy one, as it were. Now if we want a feverish city along with all the luxuries it might provide, we will need to enlarge our city. The healthy city will no longer be adequate. On the contrary, we must now increase it in size and population *and fill it with a multitude of things that go beyond what is necessary for a city*—for example, pastries, perfumes, and prostitutes. And because the land that was formerly adequate to provide for our healthy city will no longer suffice, the luxurious city must be further enlarged, and not just a little, but by the size of a whole army. For we will need to seize some of our neighbors' land if we are to have enough for pasture and ploughing. And we will need to defend ourselves from retaliation. Furthermore, in addition to the spirited and able-bodied guardians who will defend the city, we will also need philosophical guardians to regulate as best they can the unnecessary and unruly appetites which now rule in our city.

**

Yes, we each need the care of others—a need and a care far more profound than the founding of any city. A need that points not toward our indigence but toward our wealth. A care that does not merely maintain bare life but raises us up into the fullness of humankindness.

Philosophy: of agri-culture

***

Our need and our care long precede and far exceed the founding of any city. And the care for our needs unfolds into the fullness of its essence before and beyond any city. Such a care faithfully attends to our nakedness, our fragility, our dependence. And such a care accomplishes our humankindness.

***

For countless ages we cared for our nakedness, our fragility, our dependence without any need for cities and the agri-culture on which they are founded and raised up. For countless ages we cared for our many needs without any need for the logics and economies of agri-culture and its cities.

***

If need is the creator of cities, it is not the need for food, clothing, or shelter that founds them. These are provided for in abundance long before and far beyond the founding of any city. Nor is it the need for celebration, for play, for worship, or for contemplation that creates the city. For these too abound before and beyond the founding of any city.

***

Before and beyond the city our dwelling was not as poor, nasty, brutish, and short as some would have us imagine.

Of Humankindness

***

Before and beyond the city there abound ample places and occasions for thinking—a thinking in no way reducible to or exhausted by philosophers and their philosophies. A thinking not subjected to work. A thinking not dominated by the house and all it houses, by the polis and all it polices. A thinking nurtured and raised up in the labors of caring for our nakedness, our fragility, our dependence. A nurture and labor before and beyond a cult(ure) of work(s).

***

A city may be simple and healthy *as a city*—and yet not be simple or healthy as a manner of dwelling with one another upon the earth.

***

Despite any seeming simplicity, how much must have already happened before the founding of any city? How much must have been ploughed up and covered over? How much must have been forgotten prior to the founding and raising up of any city?

***

The city—along with all it holds, all it maintains and raises up—is no more necessary than the field of agri-culture.

Philosophy: of agri-culture

***

Curiously absent from the simple and healthy city: the philosopher and his philosophy. There seems to be neither need nor space for his discourse or his way of life. Such a city seems to get along fine without his form of farming, without his form of harvesting and threshing. Such a city seems to get along fine without his form of therapy, without his form of guarding and regulating.

***

Like the simple and healthy city, the luxurious and unhealthy city is founded and raised up upon an agri-cultural base.

Yet the luxurious and unhealthy city is not the only diseased city in need of therapy and healing.

***

Philosophers and their philosophies may take their place alongside the pastries, perfumes, and prostitutes of the unhealthy city, but there is a need for some kind of therapy in even the simplest and healthiest of cities. This is a therapy of tending the wounds opened up in our turning away from one another and toward things.

***

Of Humankindness

Aristotle: It is generally acknowledged that in a well-ordered state the citizens should have leisure and not have to provide for their daily wants, but there is a difficulty in seeing how this leisure is to be attained.

***

Agri-culture: a taking up and putting to work—at the expense of some for the benefit of others—of the labor through which a world opens and unfolds. This taking up and putting to work allows some to withdraw from the labors of caring for our nakedness, fragility, and dependence and allows them to concern themselves with a particular (agri-cultural) form of contemplation.

***

Philosophy is an agri-cultural enterprise. This enterprise is a taking of the between, a putting to work of the between. This taking does not take up what is given. It takes up neither beings nor being. For the given and the giving of the given presuppose a taking. This is a taking of the between, of the sharing between (us), within which every taking—including any taking as given, taking for granted—takes place. Only through and within a sharing between (us) is any taking or giving possible. Sharing opens and shares out every place and occasion for taking and giving—which is to say that sharing opens and shares out every place and occasion for all that is, including being itself. This sharing is not given. It abides between (us). It unfolds and abides in and through sharing. The putting to work of the between is a putting to work of the labor shared between us. This is the labor of caring for our nakedness, our fragility, our dependence. All work presupposes this labor. Work is the setting to work of this labor. What is raised up in and through work rests upon the labor of caring—a caring not reducible to tilling the field, to cultivating the vine, to raising up buildings.

This enterprise is agri-cultural. Although a taking up and putting to work of the between can precede the advent of agri-culture, prior to agri-culture this taking and putting to work finds no purchase on the ground of sharing. There is no fixing or making enduring of this taking and putting to work. The conditions and mechanisms by which such fixing and making enduring might be brought about are absent. This absence is not a lack. It is the fullness of sharing, the accomplishment of labor. There is a stability within this sharing and labor that is not a fixing or making enduring. It is the stability of sharing again and again for the first time in caring for our nakedness, our fragility, our dependence. Beyond the field of agri-culture, we are gathered around this sharing and caring. This is our first dwelling, our first ethos. Agri-culture is an articulation of—simultaneously a turning away from and a turning toward—this ethos, this sharing and caring. It is a setting of this sharing and caring within fixed and enduring structures and mechanisms. Thus the home is set within the house. The labor of caring for our nakedness, fragility, and dependence is set within the work of building, cultivating, maintaining. Sharing is set within taking, giving, exchanging.

It is within this agri-cultural setting that philosophy makes its start. The immediate and proximate setting of agri-culture is one of taking up and taking over the between.

Of Humankindness

The history of philosophy is a history of forgetting and neglect of this immediate and proximate setting. This is a setting in which sharing has for the most part been covered over.

***

Aristotle: Those who are in a position that places them above toil have stewards who attend to their households while they occupy themselves with philosophy or with politics.

***

The polis in which philosophy resides as a way of life and articulates itself as a discourse is an agri-cultural enterprise.

***

Those who occupy themselves with philosophy or with politics are no less agri-cultural than the simplest of farmers.

***

Although the articulation of metaphysics may have to await the polis and its philosophers, the ground for this articulation is laid well in advance of the city. In the raising up of the house, in the multiplication of things, in the bounding of the field…—in these and other agri-cultural machinations lie the constitution of the physical and metaphysical domains or estates within which the philosopher will work; in these machinations lie the raising up and ordering of beings; in these and

Philosophy: of agri-culture

other agri-cultural machinations lies the forgetting of being in (favor of) beings.

***

Heidegger: The initial great harvest first had to be brought in. Ever since that time, the history of philosophy has been threshing this harvest, and now it is only empty straw that is being threshed. So we must go out and bring the harvest in anew, i.e. we must come to know the field and what it is capable of yielding. We can only do this if the plough is sharp, if it has not become rusted and blunt through opinions and gossip. It is our fate to once again learn tilling and ploughing, to dig up the ground so that the dark black earth sees the light of the sun. We, who have for all too long unthinkingly taken the well trodden roads (*The Essence of Human Freedom*, 34).

***

But what of wisdom before and beyond the field's edge? Before any plough has yet opened the earth? Beyond the taking of any roads, well trodden or not? And what if, rather than going out and bringing in the harvest anew, we enjoyed an elemental abundance, gathering and sharing the fruits of the earth?

***

The field of agri-culture is the site of philosophy—of its metaphysics, of its ethics, and most definitely of its politics. This field lays out and establishes the first philosophical entity. It is itself this entity.

Of Humankindness

The roots of philosophy reach into the soil of agri-culture.

Philosophy is a thinking proper to agri-culture.

***

There is no primordial philosophy, no universal philosophy. Philosophy begins with and in agri-culture. It is an articulation of agri-culture, a form of agri-culture. It is a refining of an initial harvest. It is dependent upon this harvest for the material (*ousia*) it works—gleaning from a field someone else has sown. It stays within the bounds of the field of agri-culture—either threshing again and again an old harvest or harvesting anew. It is confined to this field and what it is capable of yielding—and remains largely ignorant of what the field is incapable of yielding or what the very presence of the field prevents from coming forth. It fails to see that even when it wanders down well trodden roads, far from any plough, it remains within the field of agri-culture.

***

Agri-culture: a proliferation of (durable) things; a domination of existence by things—by the house and all it houses; a colonization of attention by and around things.

***

Philosophy: of agri-culture

The field of agri-culture yields more than the fruits of the soil and the vine. It also yields the house and all it holds: *ousia*, the fixed and enduring possessions ready-to-hand in and around the house. And it also yields the *ousia*—the being, the substance—of the philosopher.

With our settled existence—our coming to reside in houses and alongside all that they house—we become surrounded by a pressing throng of beings (ready-to-hand and present-at-hand) and come to cling to beings (*ousia*, possessions, things ready to hand). These are beings that belong to us, our possessions, the beings over which we have disposal. These beings stand at our disposal because they are fixed and enduring, because they are constantly attainable and at hand in or around the house. The constant presence, the enduring constancy of these beings constitute our estate. It is the constant presence of these beings—these useful items, the household, property assets, possessions at hand for everyday use—that provides Greek philosophy with the harvest to be threshed. This is a threshing that yields their philosophical notions of *ousia*, of being.

It is only within particular social-material arrangements—agri-cultural arrangements—that the enduring presence of things at hand comes to dominate existence. Despite the particularity that founds the philosophical notions of *ousia*, the enduring presence of things at hand has been taken as constitutive of the human condition and of world(hood) in general. That which is enduringly present is taken to be most real by philosophers. And that which is enduringly present is taken to be of greatest concern to humans in general. We are surrounded by a pressing throng of beings (enduringly present) and it is to those beings that we cling.

***

Among the fruits harvested from the field of agri-culture is *ousia*. *Ousia* belongs to the everyday lives of the Greeks, and the word *ousia* belongs to their everyday language and speech. Before it is taken up—harvested and threshed—by philosophy, *ousia* is a fruit of everyday agri-cultural existence. "Philosophy took up the word from its pre-philosophical usage" (*The Essence of Human Freedom*, 36). In this everyday, pre-philosophical usage, *ousia* refers to beings that are exemplary in their being (thus holding together beings and being). These beings exemplary in their being are those beings "that belong to one, one's possessions, house and home [*sic*], the beings over which one has disposal. These beings stand at one's disposal because they are fixed and stable, because they are *constantly attainable and at hand* in the immediate and proximate environment" (36).

Philosophy thus presupposes—takes on, assumes, takes over—a regime of making one's own. That is, a regime of propriation and property. It assumes a context, an immediate and proximate environment in which what has been appropriated stands fixed and enduring. That is to say, it assumes an agri-cultural setting and setup. Philosophy takes on and takes over a particular way of being in the world that it mis-takes for being in the world as such.

Philosophy: of agri-culture

It is within this regime of propriation (appropriation, possession, disposability) that home is confused with house (and house is confused with world). It is within this regime that what can only be shared between is taken as a disposable possession, as constantly available. The sharing, again and again for the first time, through which a home is brought forth and sustained—not as enduringly present and at hand but as cared for through the sharing of labor that attends to our nakedness, fragility, and dependence—is taken as given.

When sharing is taken as given, beings come to *reside* in their givenness, their *constant availability*. "As constantly attainable they lie close at hand.... They are what is closest and in this constant closeness they are present and at hand in a definite sense. Because they are present and at hand in an exemplary sense, we call possessions, house and home [*sic*], etc. (what the Greeks call *ousia*), *estate*. It fact, by *ousia* nothing else is meant but constant presence, enduring constancy. What the Greeks address as beings proper is what fulfills this understanding of being as *being-always-present*" (36–37).

Within agri-culture things—taken as possessions, taken as that over which one has disposal—may indeed lie closest. They may lie so close that they press upon us and weigh us down. And in doing so, even as they draw (and push) us together, they push us away from one another, from sharing with one another. And away from the earth. For what, after all, are these foundations and walls, these roofs and thresholds? Agri-culture is the context in which things lying close at hand are constantly available; the context in which our sharing with one another is pushed aside in favor of dealing with things—and our dealing with one another is made to pass through this dealing with things.

Within agri-culture there can be an *estate*, a constant presence of things. With agri-culture, our attention is drawn away from sharing with one another (in the worlding of the world) and toward the arranging and disposing of possessions, of what can be possessed. It is these possessions, these things that are enduringly present.

***

The being and time of philosophy are a being and time of agri-culture.

***

The thinking of a people is rooted in the soil of its existence. And although its thinking may not be reducible to this soil, it does not altogether rise above or escape this rootedness. The soil of our thinking these past 12000 years has been an agri-cultural soil. The dependence of our thinking upon this agri-cultural soil can be difficult to discern insofar as the fruits of the agri-cultural field are taken far from it and extensively refined. And all the more difficult to discern when the fruits no longer come directly from the field but from the institutions and cities that are raised up upon agri-cultural foundations.

Philosophy: of agri-culture

For the past 12000 years, thinking has been rooted in agri-culture. Its most basic concepts are the fruits of agri-cultural fields.

Even something as seemingly rarefied as *ousia*—as being, as substance—is rooted in agri-cultural existence. The processes of harvesting and extracting, of threshing and refining begin with the yield of agri-cultural arrangements. Thus, in the everyday language of the Greeks, *ousia* means "useful items, the homestead, property assets, possessions, that which is at hand anytime for everyday use, that which is immediately and for the most part always present" (*The Metaphysical Foundations of Logic*, 145). It is within, upon, and from the agri-cultural arrangements—the logic and economy—presupposed by this understanding of *ousia* that philosophy makes its start. And it does so without ever taking account of these agri-cultural foundations—and even less so of the ground on which these foundations rest. Philosophy begins with a taking for granted. And although it may come to see the granting, it remains largely blind to the taking that precedes it and makes it possible—and even more blind to the sharing that precedes and exceeds this taking and granting.

***

Like the notion of *ousia*, the notion of *hypokeimenon* is an agri-cultural artifact. It is rooted in agri-cultural existence and raised up upon agri-cultural arrangements. It is within an agri-cultural setting that some thing is made to stand by itself, free from dependence upon and entanglement with other things. The supposed independence and self-sufficiency of the agri-cultural household is put to philosophical work. The *hypokeimenon* is said to reside in itself. It is said to be what it is all by itself, with no need of other things in order to exist. Such a notion arises within an agri-cultural setting in which things are set apart from one another, a setting in which things are disposed such that they might be ready to hand. Even when it is laid down or raised up as a philosophical concept, *hypokeimenon* retains its agri-cultural roots.

***

The foundations of logic are less metaphysical than they are agri-cultural. They are metaphysical only because they are first and foremost agri-cultural: *The Agri-cultural Foundations of Metaphysics and Logic*.

***

It is within an agri-cultural setting that there is a household (filled with possessions that can stand ready-to-hand). It is within this setting that property assets and useful items come to *dominate* our existence. The house houses useful things. Before and beyond the field of agri-culture, the world is not filled with property assets or useful items—and even if there happen to be useful items here and there, they do not dominate existence, they do not fill the world. The ways in which households, useful items, and property assets dominate our existence are particular to agri-culture. And the ways in which the world is gathered around these things are also particular to agri-culture.

**

Before and beyond agri-culture, being does not dominate existence. The world is not then replete with beings. It is not then a world of beings—or of being. Such a world is a consequence of agri-culture.

It is within and upon the existence of enduring presence—an existence particular to agri-culture (founded upon the house and all it houses)—that being comes to be experienced and thought.

**

Heidegger: When tradition…becomes master, it does so in such a way that what it "transmits" is made so inaccessible, proximally and for the most part, that it rather becomes concealed. Tradition takes what has come down to us and delivers it over to self-evidence; it blocks our access to those primordial "sources" from which the categories and concepts handed down to us have been in part quite genuinely drawn. Indeed it makes us forget that they have had such an origin, and makes us suppose that the necessity of going back to these sources is something which we need not even understand (*Being and Time*, 43).

**

The categories and concepts of agri-culture have been delivered over to self-evidence. We have forgotten that these concepts and categories have their origin in the soil of agri-cultural existence.

***

In taking equipment as what lies closest to us, and then using this as a clue for disclosing the world, our sharing-with-one-another in an ethos that precedes and exceeds equipment and the world of assignments and references that equipment discloses is covered over, thrust aside, or put to work. The world of things, the world in which it is things that lie closest is a world that presupposes the sharing-with of a more primordial ethos that this world covers over—often by putting this ethos to work in the service of its schemes and machinations. When things dominate our existence, our sharing with one another in an ethos is thrust aside in favor of things. And our being is understood in terms of a concernful care that is not primordial, a concernful care that covers over and disguises our care for one another before and beyond all things.

***

Before any region can be discovered—a region holding various estates; a region in which places can be allotted or come across "for a totality of equipment that is circumspectively at one's disposal" (*Being and Time*, 136)—an ethos must be shared. The belonging somewhere of any item or totality

Philosophy: of agri-culture

of equipment presupposes the belonging of (and to) a shared ethos in which any thing can matter to us. Before the "above" of any ceiling or the "below" of any floor, before the "behind" of any door or the "in front" of any window lies the nearness of a shared ethos. In this nearness it is not ceilings or floors or doors or windows that surround us. It is hearts and hands, faces with eyes and ears. We share the space and spatiality of this ethos before and beyond being situated in the space of circumspective concern.

***

Hand in hand with a privileging of things as what lies closest is a notion of world(hood) that is lit up by equipmental breakdowns. In the breakdown of equipment the agri-cultural world is disclosed.

But when our bellies cry out in hunger and our hands have not found what they sought, we stand face to face with a sharing of nakedness, of fragility, of dependence through which the world worlds. And the injury, the sickness, or the death of any one with whom we share such nakedness, fragility, and dependence more fully solicits—both makes tremble and calls forth—a world, an ethos far more profound than the world disclosed by the breakdown of any equipment.

***

Of Humankindness

It is a mis-take to place our sharing, our ethos—even in the impoverished sense of being-with (solicitude)—alongside our concernful dealings with things.

***

Our sharing-with-one-another is not simply an aspect, a component, a dimension of being-in-the-world. Our sharing *with* does not simply occur *in* the world. With our sharing the world worlds.

***

Levinas: …Heidegger, with the whole of Western history, takes the relation with the Other as enacted in the destiny of sedentary peoples, the possessors and builders of the earth (*Totality and Infinity*, 46).

***

Philosophy presupposes an agri-cultural ethos. It is this ethos that is articulated in everyday practices and then refined by philosophy.

Philosophy, which includes metaphysics, rests upon an ethos, an ethics. The task of first philosophy would be to discern and articulate the ethical—that is, agri-cultural—ground from which it itself grows.

***

Philosophy: of agri-culture

    Despite—and indeed even in—all the critiques, subversions, and deconstructions of metaphysics these past several hundred years, the soil from which metaphysics has grown continues to be ploughed and harvested. A nearly universal ignorance or neglect of the relation of metaphysics to agri-culture continues to reign. This ignorance has been so profound that even among some of metaphysics' most staunch critics there has been a more or less naïve embrace of agriculture (and agri-culture) that has reinforced the very metaphysics to be overturned or deconstructed.

    Agri-culture is a manner of dwelling upon the earth and with one another. Metaphysics is a form of thinking or of discourse within agri-culture. If we are to loosen agri-culture's grip upon our thinking—and, more importantly, upon our dwelling—a turn toward agri-culture is needed.

    The grip of agri-culture upon our thinking can be seen not merely in *the choice* of words and concepts within the various attempts to subvert or deconstruct metaphysics, but in the more or less naïve taking over and taking up of words and concepts—and the modes of dwelling in which they are rooted—*inherited* from agri-culture. Perhaps foremost among these words and concepts is gift—in terms of which this inheritance itself has been understood.

***

Agri-culture: a wandering away from sharing (and) the elemental and toward the giving and givenness of things and beings.

***

Philosophy is a flower—not a fruit, for it does not offer the fruit's sustenance—of agri-culture. And this flower is not a wildflower. Rather, it is a domesticated one. And more specifically it is the flower of axial age agrarian economies coming to terms with living in cities and empires (and all the ethical and communal upheaval they imply).

As a flower, philosophy privileges seeing. Its history is one of privileging seeing and the eye over touching and tasting, over the hand and the belly; favoring contemplation over labor. The philosophical imaginary—its concepts, metaphors, symbols, images; its questions, problems, and methods—these are the products of agri-cultural soil and agri-cultural work. They are raised up on the foundations of agri-cultural dwelling (sedentism, propriation, economy…). They are hinges, windows, and doors; threshold and walls; paths and canals.

***

As the soil of agri-culture is exhausted and abandoned, this philosophical flower withers and dies. It may remain—dried and pressed—between the pages of old, musty books, each a little coffin bearing the decaying remains of once living ideas. But its vital connection to its roots—roots that were never as deep, as vigorous, as hardy, as resilient as those of wild or native plants—has been severed. Can the branch on which it grows now be grafted onto other (both newer and older) plants, stocks, stalks, branches?

Is philosophy's growing irrelevance—which is not to suggest that it ever enjoyed the relevance it imagined itself entitled to—due in part to its rootedness in an agrarian economy that has been eclipsed, surpassed, abandoned? Is its irrelevance due in part to its being a relic of a dead (or dying) past? In a world where all that is solid melts into air, has philosophy's quest for permanence, for anchoring, for identity rendered it irrelevant? Are not other ways of living and ways of discourse more successful at conveying or capturing what people need (which is much more than mere meaning—and even with regard to meaning, do not other ways of living and discourse perform better in today's post-agrarian world)?

The old ethos from which the philosophical logos sprung is dying away. A new ethos is being born. Can philosophy share in this new ethos? And in this way help to give birth to a new logos and wisdom?

Coda

I. The culture that dominates the globe today is an agri-culture.

II. Only an agri-culture can dominate the globe—that is, make of the earth a globe, an *oikos* and subject this globe to its laws and logics.

III. Agri-culture is not equivalent or reducible to farming.

IV. Today agri-culture takes the form of technoscience and markets.

V. Despite its hegemony and seeming necessity, despite its apparent foreclosing in advance of the future, today's agri-culture is but *an* agri-culture.

VI. Another (agri-) culture is possible.

The Wasteland Grows

I. The field of agri-culture has been exhausted. Its soils poisoned. Its rivers polluted. Its skies darkened.

***

The earth itself has become a vast wasteland.

***

Yes, the wasteland grows. The wasteland: of agri-culture. Everywhere agri-culture takes root, the wasteland grows. And today the roots of agri-culture extend across the globe. Agri-culture has taken root everywhere. And thus the wasteland is now coextensive with the globe.

***

Of Humankindness

This wasting has indeed accelerated and intensified these past 75 years. But what we are living through today is a generalization, a globalization of a process that has always attended agri-culture. In all the fields of agri-culture, humans have striven to become the dominant force. And now with the field of agri-culture having become coextensive with the globe, human dominance is turned back upon itself in an unprecedented manner. No longer with an outside into which it can indefinitely expand, upon which it can externalize its costs, against which it can identify itself, agri-culture recoils upon itself. Having accelerated and intensified its setting upon, ordering, and arranging of the world, agri-culture finds itself consumed by its success. The mechanisms by which agri-culture hid or denied its waste are no longer available to it. Today, waste and wasting can no longer be kept at arm's length or thrown into some outside. There is no more outside.

***

The wasteland grows—wherever the logics and economies of agri-culture hold sway.

***

The wasteland grows: in asking—imploring, cajoling, commanding—that the field give out more than it would yield of its own accord.

The wasteland grows: in externalizing the costs of this increased yield upon other peoples, other species, other locales.

The Wasteland Grows

***

The debris of agri-culture's history piles up all around us. This is not only the debris of past devastation and mistakes. It is also the debris of the futures to which agri-culture has laid waste.

***

We dwell in a wasteland. And this wasteland grows in our dwelling. It grows in the domestication of our dwelling. It grows in the domination of our dwelling by things. And it grows in the subjection of sharing to the logics and economies of taking, giving, and exchanging.

***

With each turn away from one another and from ourselves, the wasteland grows. It grows in the neglect, the covering over, the attenuation of our nakedness, our fragility, our dependence. It grows in the neglect, the covering over, the attenuation of sharing in the labor of caring with and for one another. It grows when we turn away from one another even in our turning toward one another: when we presume to know one another fully and in advance, when we dispel or extinguish the mystery of drawing near to one another, when we take one another for granted.

***

Of Humankindness

    Agri-culture lays waste to the world by taking and appropriating what was formerly—and ultimately can only be—shared. When sharing is sacrificed upon the altar of taking and appropriating, the world wastes away. When sharing is sacrificed upon the altar of gift and exchange—a gift and exchange made possible by taking and appropriating—the world wastes away. It wastes away even as it is built up and made to house more and more people and things. When sharing is sacrificed the world may be made durable—and nevertheless waste away. For there is no altar, no temple, no tomb, no monument able to safeguard the (worlding of the) world.

    The world is not made secure, nor is it cared for, nurtured, raised up, merely by being made durable, calculable, disposable. Rather, the world—and its worlding—is safeguarded in the hearts and hands opening and extending between us. The world persists and abides—it worlds—in the opening and extending of hearts and hands between us. No tool, no work (without the support of a labor shared between us) can accomplish this persisting and abiding—this worlding. A world is not simply made or safeguarded by others living elsewhere and elsewhen. Rather, a world is brought forth and safeguarded between us here and now; in our sharing in the labors of caring for our nakedness, our fragility, our dependence.

    To merely take up residence in a world already there is to die a premature death, to pass the days waiting for a moment that has already arrived, to shuffle about in the tomb of some stranger. For the world is never simply given in advance. It opens and unfolds, ever anew, in the sharing between us.

***

The Wasteland Grows

There is a wasteland wherever and whenever *the between* recedes: when the world between us is filled—that is, emptied out and impoverished—with things, with objects, with commodities; when the home between us no longer abounds with mystery—the mystery of a three preceding any two and one; when our comings and goings are arranged, laid out in advance, more and more thoroughly subjected to calculation; when the love and friendship between us no longer solicits us and draws us in; when all that lies between us is taken for granted.

***

There is a wasteland wherever and whenever we conceal our nakedness, armor over our fragility, or attempt to deny our dependence. There is a wasteland wherever and whenever the actuality and possibility of sharing in the labor of caring for the between is superseded by those works that fix the between in more or less durable things and thereby attempt to hold open the between. Today, there is wasteland nearly everywhere and everywhen.

And hence, the wasteland is not limited to bleak physical landscapes: post-modern, post-apocalyptic industrial landscapes fouled with pollution; blighted inner-city neighborhoods; third-world shantytowns. These are, no doubt, wastelands. But perhaps not in the way commonly imagined. And they certainly hold no monopoly on waste and wasting away. The wasteland thrives where many would least expect it—in the so-called happy homes of the global elite filled with the latest technological devices, in suburban malls with fully stocked stores and smiling customers, in churches overflowing with pious congregants, in the bright faces of cinematic stars. The wasteland grows deeper and more profound in our denials of it, in our unwillingness to face it, in our turn toward narcotics, diversions, and dissipations in the attempt to hide from it.

***

Although a wedge has perhaps slowly been driven since our first tool use between our nakedness, fragility, and dependence and our care for this nakedness, fragility, and dependence, this dissociation and uncoupling has accelerated these past 12000 years—spectacularly so in the past 500 years (industrialization) and in the past 50 years (digitalization). We have become increasingly forgetful of our nakedness, fragility, and dependence and increasingly neglectful of sharing in the labor of caring for this nakedness, fragility, and dependence. It is in this forgetting and neglect that the wasteland grows.

***

The wasteland grows: in our hearts and in the world.

The wastelands of our hearts and the wastelands of the world grow from out of the wastelands between us.

***

Woe not merely to him who holds wastelands within. For the greater danger threatens those *between whom* the wasteland grows. And today that is all of us. We hold wastelands *within* because of the wastelands *between* us.

***

We can suffer almost anything as long as we share with one another in the labors of caring for our nakedness, our fragility, our dependence. It is when we turn (and are turned) away from one another, when our sharing becomes attenuated, reduced to taking, giving, and exchanging that we are made to bear the weight of suffering without the assistance of one another—and the world becomes a burdensome wasteland.

***

The wasteland grows—as a harrowing tremor passes through the structure and experience of belonging.

II. Nietzsche: Nihilism stands at the door. Whence comes this uncanniest of all guests?

At the door nihilism stands. At the threshold, the separating and fixing of here from there, of now from then, of inside from outside; attempting to secure what has been appropriated; turning away and hiding from those who (now) dwell nearby. It is at the door—and even *as* the door—that nihilism stands. It is with the door that nihilism is raised up and made to stand. There between us. Nihilism is not a guest who, in addition to and alongside the door, stands there. Nihilism stands there *with and as the door*. The door is a great "No!": to others, to the earth, to ourselves; to our nakedness, our fragility, our dependence; to sharing in the labors of caring with and for one another. Through and around the door we say "No!" to sharing here and now between us—subjecting sharing to the logics and economies of gift and exchange, of presence and presents.

Nihilism is the uncanniest of guests. It is most *unheimlich*, most un-home-like. The door of the house is most *unheimlich*. With the door and the house that opens and unfolds around it, the home—our nakedness, our fragility, our dependence; the sharing of this nakedness, fragility, and dependence; the care for this nakedness, fragility, and dependence—is covered over, hidden behind threshold, wall, and roof; the home is dominated, subjected to the laying out and fixing of time and space within and around the house.

***

That nihilism stands at the door tells us that we are confronted with a matter of *ethos* rather than *logos;* of dwelling (sharing and caring) rather than meaning (interpretation and truth). Our nihilism is a matter of the hand and the heart before it is a matter of the tongue and the mind.

***

When nihilism is understood as an articulation, a consequence, an unfolding of agri-culture, it is no longer sufficient to think nihilism in terms of truth, conviction, belief, or ideals. The roots of nihilism are deeper than beliefs and ideas. A people, a culture can be mired in nihilism regardless of whether they have any inkling that their long-cherished highest values are without value, regardless of whether they are at all aware that they have been deceiving themselves for centuries about what is highest or best. Their nihilism can be altogether unrelated to any pessimism or cynicism with regard to life or existence. Indeed, it can be born in and carried along by an optimistic exuberance that fills their sails, that blows like a wind at their back pushing them into new, unexplored lands. For if that optimistic exuberance is rooted in practices and material conditions that deny their essential nature (and the earth), it does not matter to what heights and into what beyonds it leads them. It ultimately leads them away from themselves and life.

It is not first and foremost into some metaphysical beyond—a supposed locus of truth, of beauty, of goodness—that we have been placing our faith (our conviction, our belief); a metaphysical beyond in which we no longer believe; a metaphysical beyond which no longer draws us forward, upward, away, enthusing our existence. Such a beyond is in no way given. It is in no way primordial or originary—or even fundamental or foundational. It is in the house and all it houses; in a whole system of economic arrangements; in doors and locks, in fences and walls, that we have been placing our faith—not merely spiritually, but materially. A metaphysical beyond is the product of these arrangements. It is in these arrangements that our metaphysics and our nihilism are founded and raised up.

***

Nihilism lies in turning away from our nakedness, fragility, and dependence. It lies in the abandonment of our sharing in the labors of caring for our nakedness, our fragility, our dependence. Such turning away and abandonment are a great "No!" to humankindness.

***

Our home has been subjected to the logics and laws of the house. And nihilism stands at its door.

III. Nietzsche: *The madman.*—Have you not heard of that madman who lit a lantern in the bright morning hours, ran to the market place, and cried incessantly: "I seek God! I seek God!" –As many of those who did not believe in God were standing around just then, he provoked much laughter. Has he got lost? asked one. Did he lose his way like a child? asked another. Or is he hiding? Is he afraid of us? Has he gone on a voyage? emigrated? –Thus they yelled and laughed.

The madman jumped into their midst and pierced them with his eyes. "Whither is God?" he cried; "I will tell you. *We have killed him*—you and I. All of us are his murderers. But how did we do this? How could we drink up the sea? Who gave us the sponge to wipe away the entire horizon? What were we doing when we unchained the earth from its sun? Whither is it moving now? Whither are we moving? Away from all suns? Are we not plunging continually? Backward, sideward, forward, in all directions? Is there still any up or down? Are we not straying as through an infinite nothing? Do we not feel the breath of empty space? Has it not become colder? Is not night continually closing in on us? Do we not need to light lanterns in the morning? Do we hear nothing as yet of the noise of the gravediggers who are burying God? Do we smell nothing as yet of the divine decomposition? Gods, too, decompose. God is dead. God remains dead. And we have killed him.

"How shall we comfort ourselves, the murderers of all murderers? What was holiest and mightiest of all that the world has yet owned has bled to death under our knives: who will wipe this blood off us? What water is there for us to clean ourselves? What festivals of atonement, what sacred games shall we have to invent? Is not the greatness of this deed too great for us? Must we ourselves not become gods simply to appear worthy of it? There has never been a greater deed; and whoever is born after us—for the sake of this deed he will belong to a higher history than all history hitherto."

Here the madman fell silent and looked again at his listeners; and they, too, were silent and stared at him in astonishment. At last he threw his lantern on the ground, and it broke into pieces and went out. "I have come too early," he said then; "my time is not yet. This tremendous event is still on its way, still wandering; it has not yet reached the ears of men. Lightning and thunder require time; the light of the stars requires time; deeds, though done, still require time to be seen and heard. This deed is still more distant from them than the most distant stars—*and yet they have done it themselves.*"

It has been related further that on the same day the madman forced his way into several churches and there struck up his *requiem aeternam deo*. Led out and called to account, he is said always to have replied nothing but: "What after all are these churches now if they are not the tombs and sepulchers of God?"

***

Our earth has been unchained from its sun. And now it strays—and we along with it—through a vast emptiness. We are no longer certain of up and down, of forward and backward. And we are no longer certain of who we are. This errancy and uncertainty are not the result of an accident that has befallen us from some outside. We ourselves have brought it about. Which does not mean that we recognize or understand our new condition, even if we have a growing awareness of it. This awareness is a mixture of enthusiasm and terror. We are simultaneously excited by the new possibilities opening before us, as we throw off the old shackles that constrained us, and uneasy about where we might be going and how we might be getting there. Whatever our desires may be, there can be no turning back. The question is whether the knowledge and wisdom we once held so dear can be of help in our new situation.

We live in an age dominated, if not quite governed, by technoscience and markets. The power of these is such that humankind and the earth itself can be said to have entered a new age. This is an age in which old distinctions, old orders, and old certainties are dissolved and swept away. The signs of change are numerous: biotechnologies rewriting (and commercializing) the code of human and nonhuman life, the geoengineering of the planet, economic globalization.... These changes elicit both optimism and terror. What is at stake is the self-understanding of humankindness. For the human condition itself—from our genetic code to our built environment to our relations with one another—is now subject to our machinations and manipulations in hitherto unimaginable ways. What is at stake is not merely this or that aspect of the world or humankind, but the totality, if not the wholeness, of worldhood and humankindness. The self-extermination of humankind—and with it the end of the world, which is not to be confused with the end of the planet—has become a real possibility. Far more troubling than the devastation and exhaustion of the planet, whether through over-consumption, bioterrorism, or nuclear annihilation, is the possibility of breeding ourselves out of existence by breeding a being no longer open to world, to mystery; a being numb to the pain and joy of transcendence; a being without history, a being unable to meet with the other; a herd or hive being, perhaps rich in environment, but poor in world. We are confronted here with the question of which understandings—and ultimately experiences—of humankindness will guide our self- and world-manipulations; which aspects and dimensions of humankindness and world will be cared for and which neglected.

It has become increasingly evident that in deciding this question of which understandings and visions of humankindness and world will guide us—and *this decision* is *the crisis* we face—our traditional humanisms are altogether inadequate. For so much of who we formerly took ourselves to be seems outdated, if not mistaken. Today, to understand who we are and how to live flourishing and accomplished lives, we must understand the biotechnological systems constitutive of self and world. We can no longer divide and limit our study to supposedly discrete realms of nature and culture. We can no longer treat technological systems as inert matter formed and manipulated by us. For we and our world are formed by the technical systems that inhabit us, that dwell within us, that animate us. And so the received knowledge and wisdom that assumed we stood apart from a nature over which technologies gave us some measure of control requires a new assessment and interpretation.

***

Of Humankindness

Though we find ourselves adrift in an infinite universe, a cold universe seemingly without center or horizon, a universe no longer closed and bound within a (comforting) divine order, we also find ourselves confined within a global closure of agri-culture, within an ever-shrinking world without terrestrial or symbolic center or horizon. Not merely dispersed and adrift within a void, we have been turned back upon ourselves—and subjected, within this turning back, to an acceleration and intensification of agri-cultural processes now devoid of an outlet. We are now faced with our agri-cultural destiny.

***

In the wake of God's death—with the vacating and dissolution of *that* pole of radical transcendence—we are confronted with the challenge of elaborating anew the ground of our sharing-with-one-another. No longer gathered and ordered in advance by an Author of existence—nor by Society or the State—we lie in a state of dispersal. We no longer belong together. Not that there should be any nostalgia for the old forms of belonging—and their dependence on a supposedly enduring hierarchal order. But the attachments we are offered in place of belonging do not suffice. They fail to lead us toward flourishing and accomplishment. They disperse and empty us. Indeed, they go so far in dispersing and emptying us that we imagine we can forego inventing new sacred games and festivals of atonement.

We attempt to substitute (shared) interest for (shared) desire, failing to appreciate how these are not equivalent—neither interest and desire nor the forms of sharing native to each.

We attempt to satisfy—and even more foolishly to fulfill or accomplish—ourselves with communities of shared attachments, mediating our relations almost entirely through things. We belong without belonging with one another.

With the loss of the old transcendence, we seem to be left with nothing but immanence. We have mistaken transcendence for the old vertical transcendence. And we have mistaken immanence for an alternative to this transcendence. We are not sufficiently disciplined in the arts of attending to one another, of attending to our desire for one another. And thus we pass over or cover over the radical transcendence between us.

Still, a transcendence abides. The irreducible alterity of each one opens and shares a radical transcendence other than the transcendence of the dead God. It is the ordinary extraordinariness of each one that offers us ways of sharing-with-one-another, ways of belonging that are more robust, vital, imaginative, creative than the flattened and neutered being-with through shared attachments.

**

Nietzsche: *In the horizon of the infinite.* —We have left the land and have embarked. We have burned our bridges behind us—indeed, we have gone farther and destroyed the land behind us. Now, little ship, look out! Beside you is the ocean; to be sure, it does not always roar, and at times it lies spread out like silk and gold and reveries of graciousness. But hours will come when you will realize that it is infinite and that there is nothing more awesome than infinity. Oh, the poor bird that felt free and now strikes the walls of this cage! Woe, when you feel homesick for the land as if it had offered more *freedom*—and there is no longer any "land."

***

Yes, we stand in the horizon of the infinite. That is, we stand with and before one another. Each holding and sharing infinite oceans of mystery. The unbound horizons in which we sail today are born of the wonder arising from the unbound mystery we each hold and share. Our new adventures in the horizon of the infinite are born of this wonder.

***

This world, our home: no blue marble, no pale blue dot. This world, our home: not an earth system threatened with biodiversity loss or rising sea levels. This world, our home: *here, with these others*. Sharing in the labors of caring for our nakedness, our fragility, our dependence.

***

Wanderlust. Might we take some strange comfort in the knowledge that our ancestors found themselves in similar adventures long ago?

We pride ourselves on the adventures and voyages we have undertaken these past 500 years. We have unchained our earth from its sun. We have crossed and circumnavigated the globe. We have "conquered" ocean and air and even the chilly vacuum of space. We have climbed the highest mountains and explored the deepest seas and even floated in airless space with only the thinnest membrane shielding us from certain death. We have crafted small and efficient toolkits—as well as huge and complicated systems—to maintain our grip on existence. We have left the comfort and safety of our native lands, reducing to a minimum what we need to survive. [Of course, *we* today have done little or none of this. These are largely the achievements of our ancestors. We are incapable of venturing much further than the corner store—and are easily lost without our digital devices. When we venture into "the wilds," we stay on well-marked and even well-paved trails.]

These voyages have required courage and cleverness. And yet how much do they pale in comparison to the courage and "cleverness" of our ancient ancestors who set out and crossed the earth without clothing, without fire, without our symbolic systems, and without our complex and sophisticated tools? We are neither as clever nor as courageous as we imagine. We undertake our voyages and adventures only after having secured adequate insurance. And even the early voyages of our agri-cultural ancestors—undertaken with toolkits so simple that we today can scarcely imagine how they did it—enjoyed technological advantages our earlier ancestors did without.

How (and maybe even more importantly *why*) did our early ancestors—with their fragile bodies and simple tools—span the earth? How were they able to do what we managed only rather recently with our sophisticated, technologically refined equipment and our complex symbolic systems? Something far deeper, far more primordial than speech, (self-)consciousness, or reason moved and guided and sheltered our foremothers and forefathers. It was the sharing and caring between them and their sharing of the earth's elemental abundance that made them much more at home anywhere and everywhere.

***

Our wanderlust emerges, unfolds, rises up upon our wonder-lust. We are primordially moved—solicited—by wonder. A wonder far deeper than any curiosity. A wonder that before being moved by starry skies above or moral laws within is moved by the mysteries we hold for (and yet share with) one another.

***

Today we may indeed experiment in all kinds of artificial environments in the attempt to learn what the human body can do. But these are mere games alongside the trials and adventures of our ancestors. They were tightrope walkers who worked without a net.

***

Plato: Imagine, then, that the following sort of thing happens either on one ship or on many. The shipowner is taller and stronger than everyone else on board. But he is hard of hearing, he is a bit shortsighted, and his knowledge of seafaring is correspondingly deficient. The sailors are quarreling with one another about captaincy. Each of them thinks that he should captain the ship, even though he has not yet learned the craft and cannot name his teacher or a time when he was learning it. Indeed, they go further and claim that it cannot be taught at all, and are even ready to cut to pieces anyone who says it can. They are always crowding around the shipowner himself, pleading with him, and doing everything possible to get him to turn the rudder over to them. And sometimes, if they fail to persuade him and others succeed, they execute those others or throw them overboard. Then, having disabled their noble shipowner with mandragora or drink or in some other way, they rule the ship, use up its cargo drinking and feasting, and make the sort of voyage you would expect of such people. In addition, they praise anyone who is clever at persuading or forcing the shipowner to let them rule, calling him a "sailor," a "skilled captain," and "an expert about ships" while dismissing anyone else as a good-for-nothing. They do not understand that a true captain must pay attention to the seasons of the year, the sky, the stars, the winds, and all that pertains to his craft if he is really going to be expert at ruling a ship. And they don't think it possible to acquire by craft or practice the ability to take the helm whether people want him to or not, and at the same time acquire the craft of captaincy. When that is what is happening onboard ships, don't you think that a true captain would be sure to be called a "stargazer," a "useless babbler," and a "good-for-nothing" by those who sail in ships so governed?

***

One of the effects of sailing on a ship of fools is that we tend to forget we are sailing on a ship of fools. We take ourselves to be heading for a known destination. We take ourselves to be able sailors or captains—with a full, or at least sufficient, knowledge of our ship. We assume we know where we are going and how to get there. But all this is symptomatic of our foolishness.

Of Humankindness

We have unwittingly set sail, leaving the land behind us. And now there is no land to which we can return. We sail on an infinite ocean. And though we know something of the ship on which we sail—a planet subjected to the rule of technoscience and capitalism (these our engines, our sails, our rudders)—we are so bewitched and bedazzled by its glittering newness that we are blinded to many of its other features. Although we continue to speak as if we knew where we are going (and indeed where we have come from) as well as how to get there, our situation is such that our old assurances and assumptions are dangerously unwarranted.

***

Our futurists—those who *forecast* the future (which is not to be confused with *thinking* the future or *theorizing* the future) and those who are *building* the future (*investing* time, energy, materials in laying out and arranging a certain future—and expecting a return on their investment)—seldom think of the past or look to the past to imagine a future. They seldom think that the past might hold the *mystery* of the future (of course, for our futurists there is no mystery—at best there may be a few *secrets* that they are on the verge of unlocking and revealing). And if they do look to the past for a vision of the future, it is often a past that confirms their presuppositions and prejudices about the present—a scientifically validated deep or big history that confirms their present desires, motivations, and machinations. For the most part, however, these futurists confine themselves to a near future already within their grasp, already unfolding under their guidance. Their claim to fame—their supposed prescience—rests on being a step ahead of others, on seeing something already present that others have not yet seen, on having access to data and information that confirms their expectations. The future they offer us is little more than a continuation of certain (impoverished) aspects of the present (which also means of the past). It is a certain vision of time (a linear notion of time; time as river flowing off) that they offer us. *But it is not clear that their future has a future.* Yet it is clear for those with eyes to see that their myopic visions (delusions) of the future in no way exhaust the future.

***

We stray through a vast emptiness. We sail on a ship of fools. And thus our *sphere of concern* grows and grows. Indeed, it knows no bounds. As our *sphere of influence* shrinks and fades.

The world weighs heavily upon us even as it grows ever more fragmented and ethereal—constraining our movements even as we move and are moved all about; constraining our freedom and creativity (our imaginations) even as we are forced to choose and decide; constraining our thinking even as we are forced to calculate and scheme; constraining our lovingkindness even as we are called to care for one another and the earth. Although the world seems to grow less and less durable—more and more likely to vanish, to dissolve—it seems to offer fewer and fewer alternatives. It may be less durable, but it remains such as it is. It is becoming increasingly difficult for people to imagine—and sometimes even to desire—another world. And hence it is becoming increasingly difficult for people to share in the labor of bringing forth a new world.

We are uprooted from place and tradition. What was once spontaneously so—our sharing in the worlding of the world—has become increasingly rare and difficult. We have paved over the places and occasions where we formerly celebrated life and in doing so brought forth life again and again for the first time. Our world is slowly winding down—in its very acceleration and massification it is consuming itself. And we have grown unaccustomed to the ways of the world—that is, to the ways of the world worlding. In becoming expert at building and maintaining a world, we have wandered away and forgotten how to share in bringing forth between us worlds worthy of being maintained.

***

The response to our situation exceeds our abilities. Yet we await not a saint or a savior or even a god to deliver us, but rather new ways of dwelling with one another upon the earth.

***

We stray through a vast emptiness. We sail on a ship of fools.

Yes, we have left the land and set sail. Yes, we stray through a vast emptiness, our earth unchained from its sun. Still, *we* sail *with one another*. Perhaps it is on a ship of fools, lost in the horizon of the infinite, straying we know not where. The old certainties of origin and destination (except for the grave) are no longer available to us. But we are *with* one another. An *ethos* abides—even if *oikos*, *polis*, and *cosmos* are falling into ruin. And this ethos—brought forth, raised up, and maintained through our caring for one another—continues to bound our existence, to hold us together and to provide a contour to our days, to the seasons, and to the years. No doubt these bonds have become attenuated for many if not for all. For the past 12000 years the bonds of ethos have been woven into the fabric of oikos, polis, and cosmos. And as this fabric has frayed so have the bonds of ethos. But the bonds of ethos precede and exceed those of oikos, of polis, of cosmos. And even as the latter fall away, the former abides. It is in our faithfulness to the bonds of ethos—the caring warmth with which we share in existence with one another, providing refuge and lighting up, however minimally, our way—that hope abides.

***

Even when unchained from any sun, sailing on an infinite ocean or falling through a great void, we do not find ourselves altogether devoid of center and horizon. For in our sharing with one another, embracing one another in the labors of caring for our nakedness, our fragility, and our dependence, a center and horizon of concern—a world—is brought forth between us.

IV. Derrida: [There has been] a mutation in the field of the political and of the community in general. [...] we *belong*...to the time of this mutation, which is precisely a harrowing tremor in the structure or the experience of *belonging*. Therefore of property. Of communal belonging and sharing: religion, family, ethnic groups, nations, homeland, country, state, even humanity, love and friendship, lovence, be they public or private. We belong to this tremor, if that is possible; we tremble within it. It runs through us, and stops us dead in our tracks. We belong to it without belonging to it (*Politics of Friendship*, 80).

***

As the plough cuts through the earth, dividing here from there, now from then, us from them, a harrowing tremor passes through the structure and experience of our belonging.

***

The time in which we live is the time of a mutation in the *field* of the political and of the community in general because it is the time of a mutation in and of agri-culture and the forms of belonging and community that have long been proper to it. It is because our experiences and notions of community, of humanity, of nation, of homeland, country, state, of religion, family, and even love and friendship are *agri-cultural* experiences and notions, and because agri-culture is coming to an end, that we are experiencing a *harrowing* tremor in the structure of belonging.

The end of agri-culture does not mean the cessation, termination, or disappearance of agri-culture. Rather, the end of agri-culture is its development and completion in and into modern industrial agri-business. As such, it proves to be the ever more thorough and efficient setting upon, arranging, and ordering of the world, of all that lies within the field opened and cleared (now coextensive with the globe), that takes place in and through industrialization and its contemporary applications of information technologies.

***

In coming to an end agri-culture recoils back upon itself, sending a harrowing tremor through the structure and experience of belonging.

***

When the earth quakes its movement may be most perceptible on its surface, but this does not mean that the source of this movement lies at or near the surface. And though we may feel the movement now, what we feel is an unleashing of forces that have gathered over a long course of time. The myriad economic, ethical, political, physiological, and environmental concerns that plague us today are indications of our being unsettled. But the source of these concerns is more profound than is commonly recognized.

The processes that have unsettled the earth and our world along with it—the processes of industrialization, urbanization, capitalism, digitalization, globalization—are agri-cultural processes. They are possibilities of and within agri-culture. They are not accidents or aberrations of agri-culture—even if they are in no way its necessary outcomes—but rather articulations of its age-old logic. And as such they are not opposed fundamentally to what may appear to be a more settled agrarian life believed to precede and exceed their all too real and material appearance.

***

The field of the political and of agri-cultural community is both a spatial field and a temporal field. Thus its mutation is a mutation of space and time, a mutation of spatiality and temporality. And, more primordially, it is a disturbance of place and occasion (for the worlding of the world).

Agri-culture now extends across the globe. It no longer has, and for some time has not had, an outside. It has gathered the entirety of the earth within its opening and clearing. Because agri-culture is now global, its mutation is global. There is no place on the globe untouched or unmoved by the mutation of agri-culture. This is not just a matter of more and more arable land now being utilized for growing a limited and well-defined set of crops. Nor is it just a matter of an unbridled, technologically and commercially advanced urbanization spreading across the landscape, colonizing more and more of the globe. This mutation is not simply a mutation in the distribution and use of space. It is a mutation in the very spatiality of space. Space now appears as agri-cultural space. Space is no longer approached with an eye toward determining whether it possesses an agri-cultural serviceability and value. All spaces have been appropriated into agri-culture in advance. Each space is situated in advance within a global agri-cultural field.

Agri-culture now extends across the globe. It no longer has, and for some time has not had, an outside. It gathers the whole of earth's history within its opening and clearing. The agri-cultural mutation of temporality that began with the ascendance of work over labor, leading to an ascendance of durability over stability, of things and a concern for things over others and sharing with others, now governs the globe. It appropriates, exploits, and exhausts both past and future.

***

With the globalization of agri-culture, it has become necessary to begin to think there is no center, that the center has no natural site, that it is not a fixed locus but a function, a sort of non-locus in which an infinite number of substitutions come into play.

The dissolution of center and horizon sends a harrowing tremor through the structure and experience of belonging. We belong to the time of this harrowing tremor—that is, to the end of agri-culture.

***

The field of the political is an agri-cultural field. And the field of the community? Do we still remember, do we still share in community beyond the field of agri-culture?

Yes, but where and how?

***

Of Humankindness

We may have entered an age in which agrarian patriotism is a thing of the past—although the persistence of nationalism and ethnic cleansing belies any clean break with this past. Our ties to land are loosening and becoming quite attenuated. Residence within a locale, a city, a region, a state no longer constitutes or defines who we are. But let us not fool ourselves by believing that our global selves are no longer agri-cultural selves. We may not be agrarian—but, then again, agri-culture has been producing non-agrarian selves for the last 5000 to 6000 years of its 12000 year history. Neither the scribe, the priest, nor the soldier was connected to the land in the same way as the peasant or the farmer. And let us not forget the philosopher, who, since Diogenes, has considered himself a citizen of the cosmos rather than a resident of some locale. What is unusual about today is the number of people whose identity is no longer strongly rooted in a place and the extent to which identity has been uncoupled from residing in or belonging to a locale. The scribe, the priest, and the soldier were still tied in various ways to place. And their dependence upon the peasant or the farmer was more immediate, direct, evident. Even the philosopher, despite his universalist pretensions, was very much the product of a national culture—with its particular history, language(s), and customs. But today, more people than ever are more fully uprooted from any one place. Still, this unsettling is an agri-cultural exercise. It remains dependent upon agri-cultural relations to the land, agri-cultural forms of production, accumulation, and distribution, and an agri-cultural logic according to which we and the world are arranged.

Our global, multiethnic, non-national selves are still very much agri-cultural selves. And the advanced modernity in which such selves are produced and multiply is still very much a part of the epoch of agri-culture—however different our age may appear from an agrarian past. It may be true that we search today for homelands that are quite different from the homelands of our ancestors. For us, the homeland is no longer a space for the good life. We no longer derive meaning and identity, solely or even largely, from our attachment to the earth. We no longer reside within spatially fixed and thick-walled immunological self-protection systems. Still, most of us remain, and will do so for the foreseeable future, rather provincial in our quest.

***

With the end of agri-culture—that is, with agri-culture's becoming coextensive with the globe, with its colonizing of every available space, with its appropriation of every outside—we move from an agrarian rootedness (in family, in place, in ethnicity, in nation) to a postmodern errancy (with many attachments, but little sense of belonging). Our experience and understanding of both the local and the global are altered.

Our home now is said to be planet earth. [Each word in this statement calls for thought. As does the fact that few appreciate how thoughtless each word and the statement as a whole is.] We may reside in a certain locale, but we are now asked and even required to think of ourselves as global citizens. We are asked to share in shouldering the weight, the burden of the world: poverty, inequality, injustice, pollution, ecological devastation.... The affairs of the world knock upon our door and intrude into our houses and homes. Our choices and decisions are weighted with a global significance. We are asked to participate—in our most mundane and homely affairs—in alleviating the suffering of distant and largely unknown others, in curbing the destruction of species, of ecosystems, of the Earth as a whole, in bringing forth a more equitable and just world. But the immensity of these tasks is far out of proportion to our powers and abilities. And it is far from clear how—or whether—we can thrive and flourish in this situation.

With the end of agri-culture and the death of God, different mechanisms, processes, and institutions have stepped in and attempted to bring order and direction to people's lives: science, markets, the nation state. And the old attempts to bestow order and direction have not simply disappeared (even if their powers are clearly on the wane): family, ethnos, religion. But none of these seems capable of providing sufficient guidance—not merely to individual actions but to the whole of our lives. And none of these seems capable of providing the conditions for a full flourishing and accomplishment of our humankindness.

***

Our ethos (our home) has been so dominated by the housing arrangements of agri-culture (the oikos, the polis, the cosmos) that we easily conflate home with house and world with planet. Our ability to discern and to articulate differences between home and house, between world and planet has been weakened (domesticated) by our agri-cultural modes of dwelling. And now we are unable to think how ethos relates to oikos (eco-nomy and eco-logy). Thus, when we are told that the Earth is our common home we are at a loss as to how to evaluate this claim.

***

Our ethos has been domesticated by the housing arrangements of agri-culture. Our most intimate relations have been adjusted to the logics, norms, and laws of an economy that was once largely confined to the margins of daily life. The gift and exchange with strangers or those whom we only occasionally met or interacted with (cared for existence with) have come to dominate the sharing that once shaped our ethos, our home, our most intimate relations. And so now we find it difficult to imagine, to articulate a sharing not governed by or reducible to gift, exchange, (re)distribution.

***

Over the past 12000 years we have become habituated to dwelling in ever larger assemblages of people and things. We have grown accustomed to thinking of ourselves as members of large associations of people (city, nation, empire, species) who for the most part remain strangers to us. We have grown accustomed to dealing with things; to having our attention absorbed in concern for things; to having our relations with others and with the earth mediated through things; to understanding who we (and others) are through the possession and use of things. We have accommodated ourselves (through architectural, symbolic, and pharmacological means) to living with a social complexity beyond our grasp and understanding. The demands of our agri-cultural existence have come to structure (to domesticate, to govern, to regulate) all our modes of dwelling, including our most intimate modes of dwelling. The logics and economies of agri-culture have reached into and structured the very sharing through and around which our intimate, everyday dwelling opens, unfolds, and is sustained. Despite the pervasiveness of this (de)structuring, there is nothing natural or necessary about it. And now at the end of agri-culture it has become possible to imagine very different modes of dwelling with one another from the most intimate to the most distant and abstract. We have only just begun to imagine how radically—and even primordially—our agri-cultural ways of dwelling might be (re)shaped by attending (through art, ethics, and religion—the labors of joining) more faithfully to the intimate, everyday dwelling embodied and elaborated in an ethos of sharing. We have only just begun to imagine how our agri-cultural modes of dwelling might be shaped not by zero-sum economies of competition and conflict but by a sharing of abundance, a sharing in which both abundance and sharing are multiplied rather than mutilated and impoverished.

***

How—in a wasting that grows ever more profound; in an ocean of information that overwhelms all sense of scale; in a world of growing attachments to which we nevertheless do not belong; in the bringing near of what (and who) is distant in such ways that all sense of proportion is thrown into confusion—to achieve some sense of bearing? How to stand under the weight of all that bears down upon us? How to set a coherent course toward whatever fulfillment and accomplishment is possible under the conditions in which we live?

***

Even the wastelands of existence hold the promise of brighter futures, futures of flourishing and accomplishment. Even the wastelands of existence preserve the grounds for a new and better (agri-) culture.

Beyond the field's edge

I. …there lies the ground for a new (agri-) culture. It lies in the humus of humankindness.

Though the wasteland grows, this ground abides.

***

Even within agri-culture, we dwell beyond the field's edge. Even within the wastelands of agri-culture, the ground for a new culture abides.

It abides in the fertile soil of our nakedness, our fragility, our dependence. And it abides through sharing in the labors of caring for this nakedness, fragility, and dependence.

***

Of Humankindness

Agri-culture is not merely the tilling of the soil, the cultivating of the vine, or the raising up of buildings. It is a profound disturbance of the ground upon which we dwell. This ground is not simply the earth that supports us or the soil that sustains us. It lies, more primordially, in our belonging together. And thus agri-culture can be said to be a tremor in the composition and experience of our belonging together; a soliciting, a taking up and taking over, a laying out and arranging of our belonging together in which giving, taking, and exchanging come to prevail over sharing; in which work and action come to prevail over labor; in which things come to prevail over the elemental; in which the manufacture and exchange of things comes to prevail over sharing/the elemental; in which our relations to one another, to ourselves, and to the earth are increasingly mediated and dominated by things (*Commemorating Prometheus*, 94).

***

It can happen that things come to dominate the world; that the sharing between us comes to be articulated around the taking, giving, and exchanging of things. It can happen that we forget or neglect our sharing/the elemental in favor of the giving and exchanging of things—a giving and exchanging that commence with taking, a taking that occurs through the taking up and taking over of sharing. There where sharing prevailed, taking and giving and exchanging come to dominate. But all such forgetting, neglecting, dominating rest upon a sharing they can in no way exhaust. This sharing abides in all dwelling—even in the most appropriative, wasteful, and destructive of agri-cultural economies.

Beyond the field's edge, the world is not replete with things. Nor is it dominated by things or articulated around and by way of things. We share a world, even within agri-culture, beyond agri-culture, beyond the field's edge. This is an elemental world—of earth, air, fire, and water; of breath, blood, and milk; of hearts and hands. These are no (mere) things. And the elemental world is not replete with things. This is a world shared between us—shared before and beyond all gift, all exchange; shared before and beyond all things, all mediation of our sharing by things. In the sharing of hearts and hands, in the sharing of blood and breath, an ethos opens and unfolds between us. We ourselves are brought forth through and within this sharing. We do not precede it, enacting it within a world that would somehow precede us. In this sharing, the world worlds. And we are brought forth sharing in this sharing. Through and within such sharing lies all place and occasion for things.

Before and beyond the field of agri-culture—a before and beyond not situated in some past, not localized in some distant, remote yonder, but rather here and now—a sharing prevails, which is to say a world prevails. A sharing, a world not absorbed by or exhausted in things; a sharing of the elemental, an elemental sharing; a sharing not of things but of warmth, of attention; a sharing of a care not focused on or around things; a sharing that precedes and exceeds the economies and logics of agri-culture.

***

Of Humankindness

The field of agri-culture may have become coextensive with the globe, but it is not and never will be coextensive with the world.

And the logics and economies of agri-culture may have laid waste to the world, but the world still abides. The world of agri-culture does not exhaust the whole of the world.

***

Agri-culture in no way exhausts the humus of humankindness. Nor does agri-culture in any way accomplish our human sojourn.

At the end of agri-culture, we do not know who we might yet become. We do however know that our agri-cultural misadventures these past 12000 years in no way exhaust the possibilities of humankindness.

***

Even within the bounds of sedentary existence, even within the wastelands of agri-culture, we draw near and share in a sharing through which a world opens and unfolds again and again for the first time.

***

There are mountains and valleys and there are deserts and swamps that do not appear on any map of the world such as agri-culture knows it. These are mountains and valleys and deserts and swamps that do not figure in the calculations of agri-culture; mountains and valleys and deserts and swamps that do not count according to the logics and economies of agri-culture.

In these mountains and valleys and deserts and swamps there abound places and occasions of wonder. There abound places and occasions of sharing and caring. And there abound places and occasions free from—if not altogether devoid of—things and the domination of things. In the safeguarding, cherishing, and nurturing of such places and occasions lies the recovery and renewal of humankindness and world.

***

In these mountains and valleys and deserts and swamps there abound ample opportunities to nurture and cultivate the virtues of uselessness—virtues that exceed the logics and economies laying waste to our world.

The more useless a people, a place, a thing appears within the calculations of global agri-culture, the more likely it is to be passed over by the forces of utility and commerce. So what are the useless, empty valleys in our own lives where we might preserve, safeguard, and nurture a world other than the world-destroying world surrounding us? Where in our own lives are the swamps not even worth draining into which we might withdraw—not merely to survive but to thrive and to flourish? For swamps and empty valleys can hold an abundance of life.

Of Humankindness

***

In the sharing of abundance, the surplus born of scarcity recedes. And in the sharing of abundance we enjoy a wealth beyond all accounting.

***

We share in this sharing before and beyond any settling down behind the thresholds and walls of domesticated existence. This sharing precedes and exceeds the house and all it houses, precedes and exceeds work and all its works. Through such sharing we venture beyond the logics and economies of any domestic arrangements. In such sharing we share in an overflowing elemental abundance.

***

We dwell beyond the field's edge—even while residing within the bounds of agri-culture—by setting out again and again for the first time on that sojourn which primordially sets us on the way of humankindness. This sojourn, this way opens and unfolds in the sharing between us—a sharing of our nakedness, our fragility, our dependence; a sharing of the labors of caring for this nakedness, fragility, and dependence. To share in such sharing exceeds our powers and abilities. It is not at our disposal, at our command. Such sharing brings us forth and sustains us before we come to possess any ability to dispose or distribute.

Beyond the field's edge

***

Though the wasteland grows, the ground for a new culture abides. The way toward this ground opens and unfolds in (the) turning toward (of) humankindness, a turning toward that simultaneously sets in relief and elaborates humankindness.

II. Turing toward—and turning away

The way beyond the field's edge lies in turning toward our nakedness, our fragility, our dependence.

And the way beyond the field's edge lies in sharing the labors of caring for this nakedness, fragility, and dependence.

***

The way beyond the field's edge lies in caring for nakedness, fragility, and dependence. It has been our neglect of this care these past 12000 years that has led to the hunger, deprivation, and dis-ease that now lay waste to our world. This neglect has been so great that today, even when we turn our attention, our concern toward addressing or eradicating hunger and deprivation and disease, we fail to care for and safeguard the nakedness, fragility, and dependence that lie behind them.

Although the flourishing and accomplishment of humankindness may require the reduction or elimination of hunger, deprivation, and disease, this flourishing and accom-

Of Humankindness

plishment lie in our caring for the unfolding, nurturing, and maturing of our primordial nakedness, fragility, and dependence.

***

Beyond the field's edge, our hearts and hands turn toward humankindness and the labors of caring for this humankindness. And our eyes and tongues follow the leadings of our hearts and hands.

***

Behind even hardened hearts and clenched fists there abide tender hearts and open hands. Such hearts and hands are native to us.

With tender hearts and open hands we are inclined toward the tender hearts and open hands of others.

***

Turning in these ways, we turn toward the with of existence—within which every "from" and "for," every "to" and "in" find their place and occasion.

***

This with, before spanning a distance between beast and god or between earth and sky, spans the irreducible mystery between one and another. In this spanning the mystery of each and all surges forth. To span in this way is not to reduce or eliminate, but rather to safeguard and hold together. Indeed, the spanning intensifies and fecundates the between and the mystery of the between. The spanning of the between draws each and all further into the mystery of sharing.

***

In turning toward the between, toward our sharing with one another, we turn away from the enclosing walls we have erected and maintained these past 12000 years—the enclosing walls that have turned us away from one another, away from the earth, and away from ourselves. And thus our turning toward is a turning away from this (agri-cultural) turning away.

***

Though we were born but yesterday, our hearts tendered by the loving care of others, we have raised up walls of stone around us, turning us away from one another and closing us off from one another. And in this way our hearts have grown hard. Indeed, there is no wall so hard or so high as a hardened heart.

Still, the waters of sharing continue to flow. And even the most hardened of hearts must now and again draw water from the perennial springs of sharing. Even the most hardened of hearts must build their enclosing walls near the perennial waters of life. For all are dependent beyond measure—and no one's fragility is cast off by being hidden behind high walls of stone.

The waters of sharing forever flow. They seep into the firmest foundation. They rain down upon the highest wall.

Of Humankindness

And there they work their wonders. For what is most gentle and most yielding opens up the hardest of stone and the hardest of hearts. Our vulnerability is exposed again and again—perhaps no more so than when we try to conceal it (*Commemorating Prometheus*, 119).

***

In caring for humankindness we go beyond what is merely given—and beyond even the giving of what is given—to share in the sharing forth of world. We share in the opening, unfolding, and sustaining of the horizon of all horizons.

***

In caring for humankindness we turn toward the irreducible mystery that forever stands between each and all and that forever binds each and all. We turn toward the mysteries of sharing, returning us to our home. This sharing exceeds the bounds of all economy.

In the home the mysterious warmth and radiance of sharing/a world abide.

III. Setting in relief

In turning toward humankindness, we find ourselves set in the relief of sharing—a sharing that already holds us in advance of our turning.

***

Within agri-culture, we tend to forget that before and beyond the cultivation of the field there abides a sharing forth of each and all, a sharing out in which all share. It is through and upon this sharing that agri-culture makes its start. And it is through this sharing that all our ways of dwelling upon the earth arise and come forth. With a renewal of our sharing with one another—a renewal of caring, meeting, dwelling, loving—we set out along the way toward a sharing that precedes and sustains agri-culture as well as those forms of exchange, of giving and receiving, of giving and taking to which our relations are subjected through and within agri-culture. With a renewal of these more primordial ways of dwelling, we can participate in bringing forth anew a sharing between us. And thus we can come to participate in that resurgence of sharing through which the forms of appropriation and mastery made possible through agri-culture might loosen their grip upon our existence (*Commemorating Epimetheus*, 26).

***

Set in the relief of sharing we find ourselves set in the perennial font of life. The overflowing abundance of the elemental washes over us, not only slaking our thirst but cleansing us in body and soul and renewing our relations to the earth, to one another, and to ourselves.

***

When we dwell near the perennial font of life, there is no need to go digging wells whether in good times or in bad.

Of Humankindness

And if we wander away from the perennial font of life, there is no well so deep that its waters will carry us through the trials of life.

***

Set in the relief of sharing, the wasteland of existence recedes. The anxiety and restlessness of existence wane. The earth no longer appears as a scene of scarcity against which we must defend ourselves by way of greed, competition, appropriation.... Set in the perennial font of life, humankindness fills and overflows with the enthusiasm and ecstasy of sharing in that covenant of peace before all wars and strife. Humankindness fills and overflows with the enthusiasm and ecstasy of sharing in the loving struggles of existence.

***

In venturing beyond the field's edge we hold open the (closed) circle of economy, not in order to exploit the earth more fully, but to share once again—again and again for the first time—in the worlding of the world.

***

Set in the relief of sharing, we find our hearts and hands overflowing with a joy greater than that arising from the taking and giving of any thing.

***

Beyond the field's edge

In venturing beyond the field's edge we set in relief our estrangement from the earth, from each other, and from ourselves. We come to appreciate how we now live at such a great remove from the elemental that we have become estranged from the earth, air, fire, and water from which we still, ultimately, live. And we come to appreciate how we now live at such a great remove from one another that we have become estranged from the sharing upon which we still, ultimately, depend.

***

Set in the relief of sharing, we do not then find ourselves in a position to take the measure of man and world—as if man and world were set in relief, standing at a distance from which we might evaluate, measure, assess. Rather, set in the relief of sharing, we stand ready to share more fully in humankindness and to care more fully for the world.

IV. Elaborating humankindness

We come into the world naked and shoeless, with neither bed nor arms of defense. In our nakedness and fragility we enjoy a dependence beyond all measure. Our growth and maturity, our flourishing and accomplishment lie not in overcoming this nakedness, fragility, and dependence but in caring for them. Our accomplishment lies not in overcoming or covering over our essential nature, but in unfolding this nature into the fullness of our lives. Throughout the human sojourn we remain fragile and dependent. To live well we must live well *with*, and indeed *through*, this fragility, not in spite of it. And thus an essential aspect of our living well lies in labor.

***

Our labor is a great school—of the heart and the hand, of the body and the soul, of the ear and the eye—in which we learn to attend to self, to other, to the earth. In sharing in the labor of caring, we are attuned and awakened to the earth, to the body, to others, and to self. In the labor of caring—for our naked bodies, for our fragile souls—our open hearts are made tender. The importance of this care, and of our sharing in it, cannot be exaggerated. All our efforts are rooted in the soil of this care. What we learn of labor—in and from labor—will flower and bear fruit in work, in action, and even in contemplation. All are the yield of our labors (*Commemorating Prometheus*, 69–70).

***

In caring for nakedness, fragility, and dependence, far from doing away with them—far from covering them over or armoring or displacing them—we safeguard, nurture, and perhaps even cultivate them. Far from wasting away, they are made more fecund. We accomplish our humankindness through the labors of caring for our nakedness, fragility, and dependence.

***

When we share in the labors of caring for nakedness, fragility, and dependence, far from wasting away the world worlds. Through these ever renewed and ever renewing labors, we share in the opening, unfolding, and sustaining of a world. Hearts and hands extend—a world opens. Hearts and hands extend—a world gathers and comes forth. Hearts and hands extend—a world abides.

***

Even in the world such as it is, there abound places and occasions for sharing in the labor of caring for our nakedness, fragility, and dependence. Even in the world such as it is, more primordial ways of dwelling abide. Mystery abides all around us—between us, between us and the world. And although it may be difficult to discern this mystery, to draw near to this mystery, the mystery abides.

***

We may be adrift on the ocean of the infinite. And the centers of old may no longer hold us and our world together. But our hearts are still inclined toward one another. A world still opens and unfolds between us—a world held together not merely, nor first and foremost, by our works but rather by our labors. And in faithfulness to one another—which is also a faithfulness to the earth—there lies the hope not merely of continuing the journey but of flourishing along the way.

V. Caring for our common home

This world, our home. Shared between us. No blue marble, no pale blue dot.

***

This world, our home. Shared between us. Not given in advance—even as shared. Opening and unfolding through sharing. Sustained and raised up through sharing.

***

This world, our home. Not merely a house—full of "goods"—we might break into, rob, possess, dispose of as we wish. Not merely a house we might inherit, take, give, exchange, pass on. A home we can only share. A home that abides in the sharing of it.

***

This world, our home. Impoverished in being taken for granted. For a home flourishes and prospers through sharing—and the taking of it for granted leads sooner or later to (its) loss. A home abides in its renewal. And its renewal consists in sharing. Although this sharing and its abiding can be woven of a material that lends them the appearance of durability and independence, those who remain sensitive and perceptive—and faithful—to sharing do not lose themselves in such appearances.

Beyond the field's edge

***

There was a time when the earth was more truly our home. But for the past 12000 years we have neglected this home, mis-taking it for a house. And thus today, when we increasingly realize that we must learn (again) to dwell upon this fragile earth as our home, we continue to inhabit the earth as if it were our house: available and disposable; fungible; subject to our will; an object, however complex, to be managed, regulated, mastered, controlled. We continue to approach the earth (and one another) within logics and economies of appropriation, distribution, exchange. We have scarcely glimpsed the sharing that will be required if the earth is truly to be our home.

***

If the earth is to be our home, doors and walls and fences and borders must no longer stand in the way of sharing.

***

With the raising up of the house and its coming to dominate our relations with one another and with the earth, our experience and understanding of home and world are subjected to the logics and economies of agri-culture. Within these logics and economies, world becomes confused with earth and home becomes confused with house. Earth is taken to be the location, the setting for world, for home, for house. Earth is taken to be the location, the setting for the affairs of humankind. And *eco*-logy is taken to be "the home" of *eco*-nomy.

But the earth can only be our home inasmuch as we share a world—no longer taking and giving from the abundance of the earth, but sharing what has been shared with us; no longer shunning or evading the labors of caring with and for one another, but devoting ourselves to sharing ever more fully in these labors. In this way, we share a world. A world to which we belong by way of sharing the elemental. A belonging that abides through sharing the elemental. This world, our home. Sustained and sustaining by way of sharing the elemental. This world, our home. The ground of all economy and all ecology.

***

Our home, this world beyond the field's edge. A world, a home not gathered by way of things or around things; a home, a world not gathered by way of work or around works. Rather, this world, our home gathered by way of sharing the elemental. A gathering of hearts and hands through which an ethos opens and unfolds.

***

This world, our home—brought forth and sustained through our sharing of the elemental. This world, our home—not some thing over and beyond this sharing, but the very upsurge and elaborating of this sharing.

Beyond the field's edge

***

Gathered and raised up by way of sharing, we find ourselves solicited by a wonder more profound than any question. Here and now this wonder solicits us—bringing us forth, setting us in motion, moving us throughout. Here and now this wonder solicits us—filling us with solicitude, setting us on the way of care. Filled and moved with solicitude, we find ourselves on the way beyond every field's edge—every horizon opening upon another horizon; every here and now opening and extending toward a there and then; every here and now carrying us toward a strange and wondrous there and then. A there and then in which we find ourselves no less at home. At home in the very unsettling—sharing—of existence. At home through caring. With these others. Here and now.

***

A wonder holding wonders. This world, our home.

Made in the
USA
Columbia, SC